There Is a Place Where We Meet

(The Poetic Journey of a Psychotherapist)

Mark Purcell

iUniverse, Inc.
New York   Bloomington

There Is a Place Where We Meet
(The Poetic Journey of a Psychotherapist)

iUniverse books may be ordered through booksellers or by contacting:

iUniverse
1663 Liberty Drive
Bloomington, IN 47403
www.iuniverse.com
1-800-Authors (1-800-288-4677)

ISBN: 978-1-4401-7117-8 (sc)
ISBN: 978-1-4401-7118-5 (ebk)

Printed in the United States of America

iUniverse rev. date: 9/29/2009

To Chuck, fellow poet and great friend:
Your kindness, baker's magic and brotherly friendship are unequalled,
and your moving poems are indeed "unfolded wings of wonder."

To my clients:
Thank you for entrusting me with those searching and struggling
moments of your life. You have all taught me so much about the
resiliency of the human spirit, and the empowering importance of finding Hope.
May you continue to discover meaning in your struggles,
have shelter in the storms, and find and maintain Hope in your lives.

To my children, Joshua, Zachary, Shayla and Brittany:
You are all amazing and inspiring blessings!
Whenever you might doubt my love,
or if we should ever lose our connexion in the present or future days,
you can always find me here, in these pages.

And most importantly,
To my beautiful wife, Martha:
Your loving and kind presence is the best gift of my life,
and our life together is the most inspirational poem I have ever read.
MVTTO!

"You have your way.
I have my way.
As for the right way,
the correct way,
and the only way,
it does not exist."
--Friedrich Nietzsche

Doc Holliday:	"What do you want?"
Wyatt Earp:	"Just to live a normal life."
Doc Holliday:	"There is no normal life, Wyatt. There's just life. Now get on with it."
Wyatt Earp:	"I don't know how."
Doc Holliday:	"Sure you do..."

-- Kevin Jarre

Mark Purcell

Contents

Introduction

There is a place where we meet in our lives that is universal, so similar in so many ways to the life experiences that other people around us are living. We live such parallel lives, beginning as a totally dependent bundle of tears and messy diapers, gradually learning to crawl, stand, walk and then run, through childhood with our own shared, though individualized, experiences of innocence and play, and woundedness and pain. We share similar experiences with education and our own personal and common areas of excellence and mediocrity, social belongingness and classmates who welcomed us, contrasted with awkward moments trying to fit in with our peers who sometimes questioned our presence. Our lives parallel through maturation into adolescence, struggling to belong and to connect with an integrated identity, to explore romance and eventually passion as we awkwardly adapt to new bodies and heightened emotions. In young adulthood, we explore ourselves in our jobs, eventually choosing careers, that fulfill us or frustrate us, usually both, or a succession of career choices, hoping to find our calling. Sometimes our relationships work and last, soaring to the pinnacle of satisfaction, and sometimes our relationships struggle and discontinue, plummeting and crashing to the valley of disappointment and broken-heartedness. For many of us, parenting comes to connect our universal experiences, as we learn to birth children, care for them, and to appreciate and finally understand our own parents and ancestors. We see ourselves in our own children, watching our souls walk around outside our bodies, while reminding our parental pride that each child is unequivocally unique, as well. Work demands and supervisors challenge us and reward us, and sometimes burden and exhaust us. Our bodies grow older, as well as those of our friends and families, and by necessity, we learn to adjust and adapt to the years that we are granted, and to find hope in the people and the moments that remain.

Like the ready-to-be-born baby struggles when the moment comes to exit the security of the womb through the birth canal to search out a frightening, unfamiliar world, so do we struggle in living, repeatedly called upon to exit our cocoons of security as we enter new territories or new phases of our lives, initially experienced as unsafe and unfamiliar. In the struggle at birth, the baby must think that it is dying, yet it is simply being born. In our struggle to live as adults, we experience various moments that feel like death which are more accurately moments of present realities ending and new situations being born. Struggling and searching, and subsequent completing and discovering are the common themes and connecting threads of these poems. There is a place where we meet between birth and death which is a place of struggling and searching. I have lived a large portion of my life in that place of struggling and searching. It is the place that has given birth to this book.

After over 25 years of working with people, and attempting to help them, as a psychotherapist, trainer, and teacher, I have not only walked through the joys and struggles of my own life experiences, and those of family and friends, but I have had the benefits and privilege of learning and living vicariously, while listening to untold hours with literally thousands of clients during their own struggling and searching. I have been encouraged by and privileged to watch the healing, growth, and transcendence from life's struggles of thousands of people, and I have felt pain and sadness in witnessing the deterioration, resistance and self-destruction of countless others. I have come to believe that the primary determining factor of whether one experiences transcendence or deterioration is a determined willingness to go **through** the struggles, and to develop an attitude: "…that looks courageously into the eye of the storm, and says assuredly: 'You will not break me…'"

Unfortunately, there are those who attempt to avoid the struggles in life by going around them, by settling for unfulfilled lives, by anesthetizing or numbing the pain of struggling through various addictive substances and processes, or by choosing a path of subtle, yet inevitable self-destruction. The capacity of human beings to self-destruct continues to astound, and sadden, me. Inspiringly, there are those who muster a determined willingness to face their struggles, to endure their struggles, and to vehemently explore any path until their searching produces self-discoveries that complete those struggles. I understand their struggling and searching for I have walked both paths, at times resisting and behaving in some subtle or overt self-destructive ways, and at times willing and determined to do whatever it took to transcend my struggles. There is a place where we meet which is a place of empathizing with the senselessness of our resistance and subtle self-destruction and another place of being stimulated by sharing our willingness and determination to move through and beyond our struggles.

In all my struggling and searching, I have had friends and acquaintances who both affirmed and questioned my experiences, helping me to realize that truly there is a place where we all meet. We meet in those places where we share common sorrows and joys, common pains and pleasures, common disappointments and satisfactions, common despair and hope, and universal struggles with similar searches. Sometimes it is on the euphoric, ecstatic mountain peaks that we meet; sometimes it is in the lonely, darkened, and sad valleys, but most often it is on the plateaus between the valleys and mountains "where distance from the valley is relieving, and the peak ahead is longingly anticipated."

As I read through these poems, written during the past three decades of my life and recall the story behind each line, I see and remember threads of sadness and of joy, of loneliness and of relatedness, of despair and of hope, of tears and of laughter, of pain and of pleasure, of darkness and of the light of discovery, of struggle and of completion, and of searching and of realizations significant to my journey here. Many of these poems, these captured moments of life, were born from my own struggles, my own searching. Some of these were written after spending countless moments with others, whether friends, family, students or clients, reflecting their experiences in vicarious and sometimes even imagined or embellished fashion. Where appropriate, names and details were altered to protect identities, though I can hardly do that with my own. Actually, all poetry, perhaps most writing, is eventually autobiographical.

On quite a serious note, one place where we meet is at the funerals in our life. Gazing into an open casket at the lifeless and cleaned-up container of the spirit of a friend with whom we once enjoyed living moments may well be the most crystal clear mirror that we ever encounter. In that mirror of mortality, we are reminded that the moments we have in this phase of our lives are limited, that the dreams we wish to realize, the relationships we want to develop, the errors we hope to correct, and the experiences we aspire to enjoy all contain an omnipresent, sometimes loudly-ticking clock, repeatedly reminding us that the time allotted to us to do all these things is finite. It is there that we redundantly discover that our hours are not endless, our days are not eternal, and that our time frame is brief during which we make our best efforts to fashion our own brand of paradise and contentment. The place where we meet is at that juncture of understanding that we work with the daylight, diligently focused on chiseling out those sculptured dreams before the sun sets on the years of our lives and we are shaken, as those around us, by the abrupt termination of our breath.

It seems that we spend much of our lives looking outside ourselves for the answers to our difficulties, for the solutions to our struggles "believing others outside me possess the light." In time, we come to realize that no person, no book, no poem, and no philosophy **contain** our answers or solutions. However, other people and the writings of others can awaken truths and awarenesses within us serving as beacons in the darkness of our own struggles to guide us to the light and strengths inside us, which have been there all along. Ultimately and with courageous determination, our internal struggles and external searches result in meaningful realizations, awarenesses, and discoveries. Our answers and solutions really are within, lying dormant and awaiting our efforts to awaken. It is my hope that in sharing these lines born out of my own struggles and searches, you may gain awarenesses and validations of your own struggles and completions, your own searches and discoveries. There is a place where we meet and hopefully, one of those meaningful places is in the pages of this book.

There Is A Place Where We Meet

I have wiped the tears of your weeping child;
You have held the hand of my dying father.
I have inhaled the breath from your first kiss;
You have stood at the altar betrothing my spouse.

I have walked through your world;
You have lived in mine.
We have cried each other's tears,
And we have leaped each other's joy.
We have celebrated each other's victory,
And grieved each other's defeat.
You understand my journey,
For you, though in different place and time,
Have walked my path;
And I understand your wanderings,
For I, though in different place and time,
Have roamed your ramblings.
I have stomped your childhood grounds;
You have gone around my adulthood blocks.

Though strangers have we been,
And strangers we shall remain,
We could in a different life
Be best of friends, closest of kin.
All lives are so thus entwined,
And all experiences so thus parallel,
That being understood and understanding
Should never be so complicated
As is far often too true.

Last week you walked with your son
Past me in the market, shopping.
You reached over to him,
Caressing his head and neck with your hand,
Reminded me of my father,
And my father's father,
And the feel of the texture
Of my own son's hair and skin
In the caressing palm of my own loving hand.
That was why, stranger and brother,
When you looked my way,
I smiled…

In The Struggles Of Life

In the struggles of life,
The shallow one has no choice,
But to plunge to depths within the soul
To find the answers hidden on the shallow road.

Tapping into some deeply internal stronghold
To grasp, against the fast approaching storm,
Clinging to the light, with darkness knocking
On the door, like missionaries with quotas to meet.

The soul only finds depth in the resolution
Of life's struggles where shallow answers
Cannot begin to touch the depth required
For useable solutions and awarenesses.

In the struggles of life,
There are no shallow conversations
About surviving when the storms
Are rapidly approaching;
We must each find that Strength
Deeply embedded in every soul,
That looks courageously
Into the eye of the storm,
And says assuredly:
"You will not break me…"

The Strengths Those Past Pains Have Grown

Closure comes to let go the ones we have lost,
When love heals the wounds from what our pain has cost.
Innocence returns to our tainted existence,
When love rediscovers us with its magical persistence.

We can release those etched memories of before,
That haunt our todays like an unclosed door,
When love hands us fresh flowers of spring,
And paints brilliant pictures of what newness can bring.

We can turn away from the pain we have known,
To embrace the strengths those past pains have grown,
When hope and love provide us the safe space within to live,
Mapping out our future that yesterday could not give…

It Could Be That You Know

It could be that you know
That piece of me I chose to show.
It could be that your guess
Is accurate of this: my mess.

It could be that what I reveal
Is beyond what even I could conceal.
It could be that how you see
Is a truer picture than I know of me.

It could be that what you surmise
Is ultimate truth beyond all lies.
It could be that what you speak
Is positive, though it may ring of bleak.

But… it could just as well be
That maybe, just maybe that's not me,
And it could just as well be
That I am still that solitude anomaly.

Thus, as I show me to you,
As much as I can be willing to do,
And as you show you to me,
As much as you can look within to see.

That we both may part from this connexion
More in tune with less perplexion,
And we both may touch those unknown spaces
Of our souls' unique and sacred places…

The Epiphany Of A Restless Soul

There are epiphanies of realization,
When all that we are and all that we are capable
Of becoming breaks through the years of obstacles,
And the fears of failure, and we are confronted
By the screams of mortality approaching,
Demanding that we locate the handle
On this life's possibilities and Fate's inevitabilities.

There are epiphanies of understanding,
When the vast chasm between the love that we know,
And the love that our restless heart yearns to know
Opens wider, whispering throughout that valley,
That to discover what we seek,
We must abandon what we know: the familiar,
Sacrificing the restlessness of security for the **chance**—
Of the serenity of contentment when the heart finds its intended one.

There are epiphanies of awareness,
When the truth that we know is all rearranged,
And the echoes of the whispers from yesterday return,
Inviting us back to some shadow of ourselves,
That once falsely contained our lives.
There is a safety in what was known,
But once we taste the newness of our souls at rest,
There is no returning to that life that was,
Lest that whisper across the valley
Becomes a roar, relentless and constant.
Truth does set us free, but the pathway to that freedom
May walk us through heavy doubts and consuming questions,
Until we courageously arrive at our souls' truth.

And these realized and understood epiphanies,
Awarenesses that shake us, rearranging our lives
Can be ignored, forgotten, lost in fears of the uncertainty of change,
Leaving us with hearts and souls still trying to speak to us
Through the restless dreams of a thousand sleepless nights…

Comes Now The Truth

Comes now the truth to shine
Her light on the lies that I
Was struggling so hard
To believe in.

Comes now the truth to remind
Me that I am not that one
That I was pretending to be;
Neither my friend are you.

Comes now the truth to change
This life of mine, meandering along
In comfortable denial of the facts
Of what is and what is not.

Comes now the truth to shake me,
To awake me to face what is real,
To make me taste what I feel,
To break me with the pain that can heal.

Comes now the truth to strip me
Of the defensive covering I hide behind,
Leaving me standing in the bare
Naked truth from which I cannot hide...

The Rhythm of Life

Today could not have been
Without yesterday's haunting wind,
Blowing by and changing my life,
Stirring up realities and other sundry strife.

The happenings of this hour
Would rightfully have no power,
Without the joys and pains of past,
Shaping and creating me at last.

Had even one conversation been altered,
Or one person or event faltered,
This moment in which I now breathe
Would not now be, as is, conceived.

There is a Great Choreographer, somewhere, someplace,
Who orchestrates my moves and your every pace,
Matching our steps in infinite, perfect time;
Then, this dance, once confusing starts to rhyme...

The Merging Of Two Lives

Miles of roads, across valleys, and over rolling hills,
She sleeps alone through restless dreams,
Anxious for a together life in that hoped-for future,
Waiting years of days for that voiced question.

Roads of miles, across hills, and through rolling valleys,
He sleeps alone dreaming through restlessness,
Anxious for that hoped-for future of a together life,
Waiting twenty years and a day to voice that question.

Two lives awaiting the moment to merge,
Too often too busy for him to kneel and find his voice.
Each day he imagines the moment, the question, and her reply;
Each day she ponders the moment, the questioner, and knows her answer.

Until one hot June day in the center of town,
He knelt with his hopeful proposition: "Will you...?"
As she smiled, voicing his perfectly-imagined reply,
Bringing daylight to his question, a fountain of hope in her answer.

Together... they drove miles of roads, across valleys and over rolling hills,
To meet beneath a cedar tree beside a river reserved for their ancestors,
On the seventh day of the seventh month of the seventh year,
Where the maker of medicine merged those two pondering lives,
Joining anxious hands and restful dreams in harmony on the Red Road...

Year End Review with Martha

Another one has come and gone,
And as my grandparents warned years ago:
Seems it went faster again than those before,
Even in spite of the extra leap year day.

The news station's best and worst review of last year
Details the same old stories of some hope and more tragedies,
As the year before and the one before that… before that… before that…
Even though this annual review twelve months ago promised differently.

Politicians continued to break promises soon after being chosen.
Too many murders and suicides failed to significantly decrease.
Countless families remain shocked and devastated by relentless
Fatal car accidents, kidnapped children, and foreclosures on dreams.

Those Middle Eastern countries continued trying to bomb and blast their neighbors
Into submission with stolen guns and insane martyrs, imagining a paradise of virgins,
As they exploded their own brains and bowels in the crowded market and across the street,
Leaving this-and-that number dead and wounded, questions eternally unanswered.

Again, American soldiers, too young to publicly consume a beer or even shave once a day,
Were given full permission to fight poorly defined wars and receive honorably earned medals,
But returned home without arms or eyes or sanity, or returned not at all… to ceremonies
That were held to welcome back those who never slept again without nightmares.

The year-end review reminded us that technologies advanced with such speed,
Light-years faster than instruction manuals or even humanity could ever keep up.
Tornadoes spun tragedy; hurricanes drowned dreams; earthquakes shattered stability.
Another celebrity divorced another athlete, as their embarrassed children headlined tabloids.

Wall Street and gas prices soared and tumbled, creating fortunes and more windmills.
Another ice cap melted another innocent animal onto the endangered species list,
Just as acres of rain forests were murdered for another tainted and greedy idea of progress,
While the fundamentalists reminded us, for the sixth decade that the end of time is near.

The local newspaper contained a year's worth of obituaries
Of expected deaths of elders, as well as the unexpected passing
Of lives just beginning their living, leaving that eternal grieving thought
Of what could have been… what might have been… and sadly, what never will.

Our older son proudly extinguished fires, earned more credentials and a brand new fiancé
Our younger son earned that diploma, his license to drive and vote, and bigger biceps,
While our daughters continued playing with dolls, discovering that boys might be tolerable,
Acne might be treatable, and to apply eyeliner without blinding themselves or each other.

But at the end of this year as the end of last year,
I continue to believe in and love she,
Who continues to believe in and love me,
And we will do so the year after this… after this… after this…

Just Another Day This Side Of The Dirt

Just enjoying another day
This side of the dirt,
That separates all of us
From a clock-stopping end
To all that has been.

Just grateful for another day
This side of the dirt,
That often pulls me downward
With mortal reminders that
Your last smile could be
The last one that I see.

Just focused on another day
This side of the dirt,
That holds me up above
The demise of dreams and plans
That must be shaped with breathing hands.

Just living another day
This side of the dirt,
Holding her hand that touches my soul,
Love healing the wounds and hurt
Inevitably occurring this side of the dirt…

Sensations Of New Times

Sensation moves beyond all that is known before,
Walking among the stimuli of novelty;
The familiar, old and disinteresting;
Darkness starving for light.

Give the man fresh tastes;
Expose the woman to terrific sights.
Listen to these sounds
You have never heard before.

Inhale the fragrance of a land
Untainted by civilization;
Feel these sensations that chill your skin
Awakening the marrow in your bones.

From the familiar, she stepped
Into his never-before world,
Hungry for nourishment
Never before on her tongue.

Savor that moment, Lady,
As a starving child,
Seated at last to a meal
Fit for the table of kings.

You may never feel this again,
But today's sensation will invade
All the tomorrows to come
And redefine all the yesterdays ever lived...

Entrance

Sometimes it is with we who love
Quite difficult to treat
Whom we love the most
In the way we so much desire.

It seems so much easier to be
Our ideal self to those who remain distant,
To those who know us least.
Yet, there are those who have grown close,
Who have demolished our smiling walls,
And our expressionless faces,
Who have stepped behind our gladness.
There are those who have had the courage to say:
"I want to meet you—
The real you,
Not just your wall of smiles,
And heart of gladness,
But allow me to enter
Your heart of hearts,
Where frowns appear,
Where concealment is unknown,
And where oft-felt sorrow takes its toll."

To those who have made entrance
Into who we are,
Who have broken down our walls,
Whom we have allowed to see
Our inner chamber of feeling and thought,
To lay our unreal faces aside,
To those…
It is easiest to hurt
And be hurt by them,
For our protection has been cast aside
In love and trust.

By our discarding this protection, we say:
"I am me.
Here I am,
Not as the person I hope to be,
But just who I am.
I am at your mercies,
For my protective faces and walls
No longer remain.

Your every action, word, look, and expression
Are analyzed in search of rejection;
Something I hope not to find,
Which may not be there.
And if it is not,
I may create it,
For in my imperfection,
I become afraid.
You see, one misunderstood move
Can crush I who am unprotected."

With those also it is easiest
To transform them into a means of relief,
Not meaning to "use" them,
But merely because there is no other one
With whom we can be as real,
As unprotected,
As trusting.

You have made entrance into me…

Watching The Years Shed Their Skin

From the tomb of an unknown life,
I watched the years shed their skin
Quietly, beneath the setting and rising sun
That left me dizzy from its spinning
Around the days that sped by in a blurry haze
Of possibilities and opportunities... missed.

More quickly than a beaming first grader
Impressing his grandparents with how correctly
He recites his newly learned ABCs,
The days of each month counted themselves off:
One, two, seven, fourteen, twenty-one, thirty;
Turn the page.
Start again, live fast, count quickly.
The sun is racing; years linger slowly no more.

I've waited several times on a beach or mountain,
Just before dawn, with the Creator and a camera
For the slow sun to rise to color the cloudy horizon,
To capture a new day's birth at the crowning and delivery.
I recorded those moments, returned to my busy world,
And within minutes, the sun was setting,
Drawing the curtain on another chance to get it right,
To do it better this time; to savor those tastes of life.

These years are passing before me at the speed of life,
And I am fastened too securely into this roller coaster;
No longer a teenager stuck at the top of the peak,
Endlessly awaiting that exhilarating decline into speedy curves.
This roller coaster ride, over four decades long
Speeds by, returning to the beginning...

Unbuckle me now!
I want another ticket;
I want another ticket.
Start this ride again.
I'll not hold so tightly this time.
I'll not shut my eyes when I'm afraid.
I'll make more efforts to get to know
The one who sits beside me.
And, rather than looking ahead for what's coming,
I'll savor the decline as we drop,

Taste the curve as we curve,
Enjoy the ascent as we climb,
And smell this joyful wind
Blowing by, reminding me:
That I am alive...
Today!

I must taste and savor these moments
While they are still in my mouth...

Through A Dark Abyss

On the edge of a cavernous abyss, he stood peering into the darkness,
With a background of burning bridges,
Too late to go back, too afraid to step forward,
Lest he sink into a blackness, consumed in a pit of unscaleable walls,
And never stop falling through impermeable darkness.

Behind him lie the deserted ruins of forsaken paths and treasureless quests,
Friends and lovers, disappointed and disappointing,
And stored wisdom useless to comprehend the midnight.
What sadistic god had brought him here,
Created and abandoned to a darkened struggle?

He possessed no outline for the abyss,
No guide to carry a light before him.
He must go alone; he must risk never returning;
These things he knew.

He considered death to hush the fear, and avoid the darkness he must pass through;
Pondered returning to a familiar world, but it held no answers to his elusive
questions;
Contemplated sitting on the edge, to reminisce the journey that led him there.
He could pray the departure of this blackened place.

When alternative considerations failed him,
He breathed a prayer to his distant god,
And leaped into the uncharted blackness.

Floating through this thick darkened space,
Unsure if he passed through darkness or it through him,
He breathed in trust and exhaled all madness,
And fell gently in sightless, soundless passage.

Time became meaningless, as he wondered: Would this darkness be eternal?
In seconds, he traveled years through blackened despair,
Until as abruptly as it swallowed him, the darkness ended,
In light too bright for once sightless eyes to see.

On the bottom of the cavern's depths, he planted cautious feet.
Eyes adjusted first to firm and sure earth beneath him,
Uncertain if his darkened plunge was now complete.

Suddenly, out of the darkness above, came a soothing strong voice:
"My creation of you began in your struggle to be born;
My creation of you continues in your struggle to live.
Out of this despairing hole, you must now climb,
Never to return here, never to forget it.
Into the abyss of a thousand midnights,
You had to pass
To meet the one,
Who holds the answers
That have eluded you."

Then, the darkness above him vanished, leaving only light,
And looking around the cavern's sides,
He saw only a strong rope leading out,
And his own reflection in every mirrored wall.

The only way out of darkness:
Faith in himself and the Source,
And courageous willingness
To face and go through the darkness…

The Gift of Pain

It is painful to be alive…
Our pain gives each of us our own uniqueness.
Your pain is what makes and will make you the unique one you are.

From your pain, you will discover who you are,
And who you want to become.
Your pain will teach you the cherished truths,
That from books and others' lectures, you would soon forget.

From your pain you will grow
Into that unique and special one
That the Infinite Wisdom always had in mind for you to be.

Your pain touches the lives of others,
For it pains them and reminds each one
Of their own special times of pain.
Your pain gives those who love you
The chance to encourage you,
To nurture you,
To stand by you,
To accept you,
And to love you.

Your handling of your pain speaks to others
Of your strength and courage.
Your tears tell us of your pain.
They are not an expression of weakness,
But rather an expression of pain and strength,
In being brave enough to say:
"I hurt and I need you."

Someday when the pain has passed,
And healing of body and soul is complete,
You will have a story,
A story of your pain,
A message of survival
That will teach and speak to others.
You can speak of the Source of your strength:
The Great Comforter and the family and friends
He has provided to make your strength complete.
Your pain will make your message credible,
And they will listen,
And they will learn from your story.

Hard truths often can only be realized
When the pain has finally ceased,
And you stand in the dawning,
Looking back on the darkness of your pain,
And see clearly that,
Though inevitably other pains will come,
This pain has passed,
And what others said is indeed true:
Our own unique pain is our special God-shaped cocoon,
From which we emerge into the beautiful butterfly
That the Creator always envisioned us to be…

Darkness Dies With Each New Dawn

There is a love that cures a man; another that destroys his vision.
There is a path that empowers a man; another that requires no decision.
There is a love that destroys a man; another that perfects his vision.
There is a path that restricts a man; another that fuels his ambition.

There is a birth that sustains a man; another that grows into pain.
There is a past that smiles a man; another that drives him insane.
There is a death that kills a man; another that lets him live.
There is a prison that holds a man; another that freedom gives.

I will murder myself slowly no more,
Crash the walls and walk free from my own prison's door
Let me walk with the living and the free
With time for you and time for me
And when my doubts and fears are gone
Darkness dies with each new dawn…

Healing Understanding

The scars over the wounds of childhood
Heal differently, remaining tender
Years beyond those wounding moments,
Ever tender scars across soul-betraying wounds.

Many spend years roaming through life
As the walking wounded, restraining tears,
Hiding the pain in shoeboxes of shame
Within closets of embarrassment.

Many spend years frightened of others,
Fearing rejection when shoeboxes empty,
Fearing closeness lest it only be an illusion,
Closeness hiding a demon dressed in angel's wings.

Many sleep nightly with dark histories
Kept at bay with lights that never shut off,
Resisting sleep, not wanting again to visit the
Dark dreams that come as reliably as the dawn.

She often wondered why he loved her so,
Yet there were so many reasons
Beyond her beauty, beyond her seductive charms,
In addition to her gentle soul and a poet's heart.

He loved her because she knew his pain,
Not as an outsider sympathizing with sad stories.
She had elsewhere lived those wounding moments,
Carrying within her tender scars over thoughtless wounds.

In the autumn of that year as the sun set,
He held her near in the dimly lit darkness;
Her pain also known and understood by him,
Loving each other with the healing understanding
That only scarred and wounded souls can provide...

Remembered Her Childhood As A Tear

She remembered her childhood as a tear,
Falling endlessly down cheeks of fear,
Dropping on distant pictures of yesterday,
Tattered reminder albums of time so far away.

Ghosts haunted her long since past;
How long, how long would her yesterdays last?
Bruises remembered, scars remain,
Continuous reminders of yesterday's pain.

Yet she believed in a day when she could live free,
No thoughts of the madness; only beauty to see,
When life would look better; wounds would be healed;
She'd walk with fawn innocence through serenity's field…

After Hearing My Lover's Pain

Rage rumbles in my mind;
Vengeful fantasies make me blind.
Harm came to her some time ago;
My love toward her is all I know.

Scars from her past sadden me;
So much pain in her history.
I listen to her stories of how she survived;
I see the strength from pain she derived.

Hatred grips my heart in a relentless vise;
He must pay for his sins a very high price.
Rage rumbles in my mind;
Adoration for her makes me blind.

Justice will visit him in time someday:
I tell myself this, but desire for vengeance stays.
The pain he delivered will come back around,
But my vengeance won't rest until he's under the ground.

I spoke to the Grandfathers on a full-moon night;
I prayed for release from this hatred so bright.
The universe will right itself without my assistance;
Belief in that truth: my vengeance's only resistance...

The Promise Of Change

And so it is, that life occurs
In seasons and cycles.
We all have known winter's loss and sadness,
Unbridled passion like summer's sweaty heat,
Fresh starts and new beginnings, green as spring,
And colorfully aged maturity harvested as autumn.

Yet the dreary winters end with springs of new discovery,
And spring's growth yields to the energetic climacteric summer's
Heat relieved by the calm cooling wisdom of fall,
And autumn's maturity moves forward into winter's call to survive.

Seasons come; seasons go.
Phases stop; phases flow;
Cycles begin; cycles end;
So hard at times to comprehend.

Security and fear rest in the promise of change:
That the NOW we know will eventually rearrange.
Our greatest pleasures and darkest pains
Reside in the promise of change:
That the NOW we know will eventually rearrange…

This Interlude Between Eternities

And the ocean tide ebbs away from the moistened beach,
Pulling its most precious shells and horrible debris back into itself,
Reminded her of life handing her its gifts and struggles,
From the innocence of the cradle to the finality of the casket,

When the closing of a life is the Earth reclaiming a part of itself,
Created of dirt and given a brief interlude between eternities
To either make the best creation from the lowliest of materials,
Or to thrash about aimlessly, accomplishing little during that interlude.

Her time above the dirt yielded pockets of pain, fashioned by the disregard
Of caretakers, too absorbed in their own aimlessness to understand
That the nurturing of innocence is sacred, fragile as a butterfly's wing,
Which once crushed, will struggle to fly for years of the interlude.

Connecting with another heart left her breathless with longing
To mend those pockets of pain, that life left behind, struggling to fly again
When shambled dreams were tossed about like hurricane leftovers,
And the touch of love calmed the storm, stabilized her flight, unshambling those
dreams.

And on that day, she walked along the shore; ocean tide flowing in to moisten the
beach,
She stooped, picking up a precious shell, cutting her finger on the jagged edge;
Walking further, pushed unsightly seaweed aside with her foot, uncovering a perfect
seashell.
Sometimes the gifts of life are a struggle; sometimes the struggles of life become the
gifts…

Similar Paths

In vulnerable disclosure,
I am safe with you
Impressed with the intuition
That knowingly
You would not hurt me.

You have walked similar paths
In similar woods
As those I have trod.
You are familiar with my journey;
I am familiar with yours.

In together moments,
A kindred spirit is shared.
In silence, we converse,
And in talking, we connect.

Often in relating,
There is a striving to "be" something.
It is enough for you and I
To simply "be".
At present, we need no defining;
No tacky labels or hopeful predictions are necessary.

In the midst of seemingly present ambiguities,
And possible future pain,
I am content in knowing:

That as we journeyed similar paths
In similar woods,
Our paths have crossed…
And now we know moments
Of walking together…

Those Words

Neither of them
Is yet willing to say
What they both so strongly feel.
In tender moments,
The words almost slipped out
So naturally,
Not from obligation,
Not from a passing moment of passion,
Not even to echo
Those unspoken words from her,
Which, as he,
She feels,
But risks not to speak.
To say those words
Is to risk hurt,
To risk him not being prepared
To hear them;
To risk his not being ready
To say them to her,
Even though he feels as she...
In quantity,
Their time has been short,
Yet they are each
Known to the other
In ways that usually
Only in years is discovered.
So he will wait
To tell her
What they both so strongly feel,
Unless at some moment,
When the feeling is so present,
So natural,
And so felt,
That with little forethought,
The words sneak out
Spontaneously voiced.

There are times,
When they lock into
Each other's eyes,
That he wonders
How deeply she can see.
There are times,

When they gaze past
Each other's eyes,
That he wants her
To see in his,
Those words he believes
He reads in her eyes...
Yet, he shall try to wait
To tell her
What they both
So strongly feel,
But in time
She will know
And she will
Reply in kind
As she hears:
I love you...

Rain Fell Misty This Morning

Rain fell misty this morning.
I watched you go away.
The skies held a mixture
Of blues and melancholy gray.

Darkness came early this evening.
I called you on the phone.
The star and moon light penetrating,
As I had never known.

Dawn came like thunder this morning.
I awakened without you.
The dew still drying on the grass
From the night's residue.

Wind blew softly this day.
I wonder what we will be.
Leaves floated slowly to the ground,
Landing close beside the father tree.

Twilight appeared silently this night.
I will see you soon.
Clouds partially blocked the light
Of the distant star and moon...

I Feel Hope Slip From Me

I feel goodness slip from me
As evil takes its stead,
And each path walked upon
Wreaks with momentary dread.

I feel hope slip me
As pain takes its stead,
Pleasures that once were felt
From no longer am I fed.

I feel serenity slip from me
As tension takes its stead,
Things I once was calm about
Keep eyes open nightly in my bed.

I feel intimacy slip from me
As isolation takes its stead.
Those once connected with
Are to me, as I to them, dead.

I refuse allowing fulfillment to slip from me
Or emptiness to take its stead.
This lack of firmly grasping life
Shall slip from me
As I remove this noose around my head…

Naturally Alone

Feeling alone comes natural to me,
When my only company is the sound
Of crackling wood burning in my stove
On a breezy, wintry night.

Even amid a crowded room,
Feeling alone comes natural to me,
When I am known by few,
And few are known by me.

On a night when crackling wood
And a still, wintry night
Are intimately shared by another,
Feeling alone comes natural to me
With neither risking first the removal
Of comfortable, safe facades.

Having mortared myself in,
Over time and tiresomeness
From bandaging emotional wounds
Caused by intimates' blows,
Feeling alone comes natural to me.

Yet, I dislike and fear aloneness:
Dislike in forfeiting the merging of my spirit
With another in authenticity and trust;
And fear as I wonder if the mortar
Has hardened beyond removal…

The Life That Was

All around me sit memories of a life that was:
Moving-van boxes filled with wedding gift dishes,
Used for hundreds of meals and dining table discussions;
Boxes of honeymoon and anniversary souvenirs;
Pictures of shared laughter and past events;
Tapes and albums of mutually enjoyed music;
Books of classroom and poetry dog-earred
To mark informational and inspiring pages;
Framed pictures bought or received,
Sitting on a worn carpet roll carefully selected,
When she was in the life that was.

I was not part of her then;
Nor was she of me.
Known only to her are the stories behind this memorabilia.
Some she shared when queried, albeit with reluctance;
Others she reserved, sitting in quite repose
With a retrospective gaze, perhaps silently reliving
A memory behind the boxes of a transplanted life that was.

Was she drawn back by these reminders? Is she still?
Did she know happiness, passion, or love yesterday
That she and I may never find in tomorrow's pursuit?

How I wished to fashion memories with her,
Build dreams, cross bridges, traverse paths,
Collect dishes and souvenirs, capture moments on film,
And choose music and carpet colors,
That only she and I would share,
To be in years to come
Delightfully reminisced by us alone.
I wanted to build our own unique culture
With secure and lasting memories,
And never awaken some morning without her
In a small, strange apartment
Filled with moving-van boxes from
A life that was…

Friends On My Bookshelf

And the books sit like monuments,
Hugging each other tightly upon my shelf,
Dog-earred and yellow-paged tokens
Of places I have been,
Lives I have lived,
Professors to whom I have listened,
Mentors from whom I have learned.

And the books sit like friends,
Leaning against each other,
Holding me up
Through years of changes;
Cradled on my lap for comfort,
Nestled near my face for guidance;
Ever willing to speak,
Endlessly patient to teach,
Awaiting only my time to listen.

And the books sit like ambassadors,
Representing their writers,
In solitude created their truths,
Composed their experiences,
Recorded their wisdoms.
Thoughtful faces I have never seen,
Writing hands I have not shaken;
Dear friends who touched my life,
But never graced my path,
Yet here represented as monuments,
Sitting like friends on my bookshelf.

And the books sit
As I walk by them,
One more evening,
Switching the lights to dark,
Retiring to dreams,
I whisper my gratitude
To friends that sit
Like monuments
Of me
On my bookshelf…

Standing On The Edge Of Thirty

Standing on the edge of thirty;
Closing the door on a decade of preparation,
Prepared by classrooms and term papers;
Job promotions and career redirections;
Equipped through joys and struggles of marriage and parenthood;
Tested by conflicts and loneliness in divorce, child visitation,
And several one-man apartments;
Taught priceless lessons by the embraces and good-byes
Of countless friends, lovers, and acquaintances;
All preparation to stand on the edge of thirty.

Too young to feel old;
Too old to feel young.
The mirrored face that returns
My gaze has changed:
My hair has moved backward
As these years have moved forward.
High school and college are dusty yearbooks on my shelf
Filled with black and white pictures of a distant boy becoming a man;
And the script I have lived
Is not the script I imagined
A decade ago.
Often have I wondered lying in my bed
In that pre-sleep stillness of midnight,
When life's truths are most difficult to deny,
I have wondered whose play I was starring in;
It can't be mine.

Standing on the edge of thirty:
My eyes are older now,
Not seeing as they once saw:
Youthful idealism tempered with cynicism;
And deeper compassion, born from experiences of loss and grief.

Standing on the edge of thirty
With an older body and a stronger spirit,
I welcome this new decade
With the preparation of experience and knowledge
That on good days I sometimes label wisdom.
I welcome it with more readiness;
No longer a lowly freshman
In an unfamiliar high school;
No longer a rookie to adulthood
Having fulfilled some apprenticeship in youthfulness.
I welcome it with hard-learned lessons
From a decade of searching and revelations;
A decade of struggling and completions.

Now through older eyes I see
And life looks different now to me;
My eyes still have years to grow,
To see in ways I cannot now know.
Someday… if my script so allows,
I will be standing on the edge of forty,
Or sixty or by chance even ninety,
With new realizations and re-evaluations,
And probably I will re-read these words
About "Standing on the Edge of Thirty",
And think to myself silently or aloud:
"Ah, what did he know?"

Perhaps You Lived Before

Perhaps you lived before,
And as a child fled with your mother
From a home grown bitter with anger and deceit.
In the fleeing, you did not survive,
And in your youth, life ended.

You have returned now, allowed to live again.
Unknown to you are the memories of your first youth,
When time expired before your dreams
Were even clearly conceived.
So you hurry now, dreaming quickly,
Toiling tirelessly to reach them,
Unknowingly wondering if time will end too soon again.

I looked at you last evening,
When our calm discussion turned angry,
And just for a brief moment thought I saw
The eyes of a frightened child,
Perhaps unknowingly re-feeling the bitterness,
The fleeing, and the fear of the end.

Perhaps you lived before,
And as a princess ruled with your prince
In a virtuous kingdom filled with riches and compassion.
The kingdom was threatened by intruding adversaries,
And your prince arose to lead the brave cavaliers
To protect the cherished kingdom.
You kissed him tenderly as he parted,
And wept bitterly when he did not return.
Left to rule alone, you gathered your courage,
When filled only with lonely consternation,
And led your kingdom once again to strength and alliance,
Serving your remaining years alone.

I looked at you this evening,
And for a brief moment I saw
The elegance of a princess,
The charm of your power,
The grace of your presence,
And the sadness of one left to walk alone.
You clung to me as I parted,
Bade me promise to return,
And wept tenderly as I drove away,
Unknowingly doubting that I would return,
Wanting never to meet abandonment again.
When I fulfilled my promise,
You passionately welcomed me with gratitude, amidst fear.

Perhaps you did live before,
And perhaps I knew you then as now--
I was the father, who mourned his daughter's passing,
And I am the kingdom guardian allowed to return...

Within A Dream One Morning

So much of life goes unfinished:
Conversations not completed,
Relationships interrupted,
Business not conducted,
Projects and goals set aside,
Collecting the dust of fatigued ambition
Like my hand reaching to touch yours,
Draws back a fistful
Of empty air.
There was so much more I wanted
To say to her then
In those stolen moments of time.

We can never remove anything
Beyond placing it within ourselves.
He shut the window and the breeze,
Darkness fell like thunder
Through all the forest's trees.

Within a dream one morning,
When the thundering dawn still slept,
I met her one time
Beneath a neon banner,
Sitting in a corner booth
Inside an unfamiliar diner,
Where the homeless go to sit
And drink bottomless coffee all day
With the panhandled pocket change
From a stranger's generous disregard.

We sat among them speaking of lives we've lived,
And those we've imagined
In the darkened dim of Tomorrow.
We spoke of children blooming into people,
And of mothers and grandfathers who
Stepped through the portal
Of their life's completed circles.

At home among the homeless,
Until the thundering dawn shattered
The dream I thought I was living...

Believing And Doubting

I am perhaps the most confident, insecure man I know,
At times appearing to others as strong, knowing, and stable,
Within overwhelmed by my own weakness, ignorance, and fragility.

There are hours and days, but most often only elusive moments,
When I deeply believe in my capability to be and to do anything I choose:
No task is too difficult;
No circumstance is beyond my coping;
A perfect relationship is within my grasp;
And I would not hesitate to ask a queen to dance.

There are hours and days,
But most often only inescapable moments,
When I doubt my capability to be or do anything worthwhile:
Signing my name is an exhausting undertaking;
Selecting the right shirt is too much to handle;
Getting along with the most congenial woman is impossible;
And I would fear rejection to ask my mother to dance.

How can I be simultaneously
So confident and so insecure:
Believing in and doubting me
In the same moment?
This seems true:
My ability to do,
I rarely doubt,
Yet faltering faith
Shadows
My sense of
Being…

Stabs In Fury

In the fury of her madness and words,
Part of me died last night,
Bleeding profusely inside with the great fear
That every cutting word screamed
Was the unclothed truth that only
Uninhibited anger could proclaim.

When the fury was over and the anger subsided,
Her love returned to retract the daggers,
But even though the razor-sharp knives were extracted,
Still I bled from the gaping, irreparable wounds.
Her reassurances that the rageful words were false
Could not erase the etched memories of her tirade.

In the bleak moment of last night's darkness,
The part of me that had faith in her love
Lost its grasp on the elusive truth.
Should I this morning believe the enveloping hatred
And desires to leave screamed in a rageful instant;
Or should I this morning believe her forever love
And desires to remain, uttered in calm remorse?

She said I had hurt her;
She only wanted to hurt me, too.
Her intended goal is now complete.

But knife wounds with small band-aids bleed still...

Peaks, Valleys, And Plateaus

There is a place where we meet
That anger and rejection cannot enter,
Encircled with warmth and connexion.
When we are there, I am safe,
And contemplations of distance are unknown.

There is a place where we meet
That love and intimacy cannot enter,
Encircled with sadness and resentments.
When we are there, I am pained,
And memories of connexion are unrecalled.

There is a place where we live
Between these extremes,
Where comfort and security sporadically enter,
Encircled with ambiguity and contemplations.
When we are there, I am wondering,
If the places we meet for love or battle even exist.

A sense of unreality permeates extremes;
Neither intense intimacy or disconnexion appear authentic.
Doubting what I most and least desire,
Perhaps I unintentionally sabotage both,
To return to more familiar ambiguous wonderment.

Perhaps life and love cannot be lived in peaks and valleys,
But rather on longer-lasting contemplative plateaus,
Where distance from the last valley is relieving,
And the peak ahead is longingly anticipated...

A Sentence In My Life

My life is a shelf of detailed books:
Chapters in common
With time's happenings,
Paragraphs of stories
That could have been,
Some that were.

You were a sentence
In my life,
Full of commas
And question marks.
You were a line,
That would not rhyme,
A paragraph dangling
From a chapter in my life
Where you did not belong,
And neither did I.

I now close that book
With its disconnected chapter,
And your sentence
From which
I am now free…
Period.

The Magic And Illusion Of Love

From your eyes,
The magic has faded,
Those eyes that once sparkled
With the mesmerism
Of newfound, long-awaited passion.

From prolonged, agonizing conflicts
And worn-out discussions of unresolved problems,
The magic has faded,
Replaced by fear and discontentment
In your soft, sad eyes.

I cannot look at you,
Waiting and hoping,
Longing for the passion to return,
And fill your eyes with the story of our love:
Once new and fresh and pure,
Like the first snow in early winter
That covers the dead, fallen leaves
From a tiring, difficult autumn.

Perhaps our passion has faded;
It seems passion always fades,
And the magic in your eyes
Was only a temporary illusion.
Is not all magic merely an illusion
To entertain and amaze an audience,
Until they clap their hands and exit,
Never forgetting the magician,
Forever remembering the magic?

I was your audience;
Your eyes, my magic.
Mistakenly, I erred as most
Watchers of magicians:
I believed your illusion was real…
Now I must applaud you,
As the curtain falls between us,
And we must each find our exit,
Forever remembering the magic in your eyes,
And the illusion in mine…

Apartment Cleaning Of A Single Man
(or My Bathtub Used To Be White)

Walking in my apartment one night,
I tripped over my shoes, as I turned on the light,
Which I wanted to turn off again, as it illumined the room,
Filled with unopened bills, two-day-old dishes, and other assorted gloom.

I let go my briefcase in its familiar spot,
And wondered how I could live in such a messy lot.
I unloaded my pockets to unshed my day,
On the dining table, pushing a crusty cereal bowl away.

I glanced at the living room, and unleashed a sigh,
At the unemptied ashtrays, scattered books and half-eaten pie.
I finally found the TV Guide with coffee-stains three,
And sat down to wonder how I could continue living with me.

Then, I walked in the bathroom to allow my bladder to gush,
And felt a little bit pleased; at least, the toilet had been flushed,
Until I peeked around the shower curtain at a most horrible sight,
As I sadly remembered: my bathtub used to be white.

I washed my hands with a small sliver of soap,
In the somewhat hairy sink, while wondering how other single men cope.
I picked up two towels from the dirty bathroom floor,
And uncovered the T-shirt worn just two days before.

I entered my bedroom with clothes on the floor,
Automatically draping yet another shirt on the knob of the door.
My bed was not made, quite disheveled, too.
So I thought about cleaning, as I usually do.

Slowly at first, the carpet I could see,
As I hung clothes in my closet, where they were supposed to be.
I emptied the ashtrays, and sorted unopened mail,
And wiped off the counters of a sticky, probably grape juice trail.

I cleaned up the bathroom sink from its hair and soap-grime,
And re-checked to be sure I had flushed the toilet from the last time.
I made up my bed and fluffed up the pillows,
And tackled my bathtub with big cans of Comet, using a least four Brillos.

Entering the kitchen, I found dirty dishes galore,
Using a knife, I de-crusted them which got even more crumbs on the floor.
Finally, I loaded the dishwasher, filling it with Cascade,
And seriously wondered how much a weekly cleaning person would ask to be paid.

Don't misunderstand me; my apartment is not always unclean.
Before guests arrive, my housecleaning skills are something to be seen.
Apart from that, I have no pets, and I'm really not home a lot,
But I do clean my apartment, at least once a month, whether it needs it or not...

Those Damned Overdue Bills

Look, look, what do I see?
A bunch of collectors who want their fees,
Endless streams of bills in the mail,
Annoying callers make me weep and wail.

"I'll send it soon," I said,
"No blood from a turnip can be bled."
"Bills are high; income is low,
That's hard to juggle, don't you know?"

They act so nice, but bug me to no end;
Some speak as Hitler; some pretend they're my friend.
"I'm trying my best," I explain to them,
"Just understand this: I'm way out on that debt limb."

"Okay," they respond, "so when can you pay,
This overdue bill; we can no longer delay?"
"I don't know," I reply, irritation in my voice,
"I'm all out of green and you weren't my first choice!"

"Well, just do your best and pay as soon as you can,
And let this overdue bill get no more out of hand,
Or we'll send you to court and force you to pay,
Thank you, dear Debtor, and have a nice day."

So...that night as I lay down on my bed,
Thoughts of overdue bills filled up my head.
"Dear God," I prayed, "Help me this problem to fix,
Just guide my lottery purchase to those perfect six."

Then, I'll settle these bills once and for all,
And no more will they mail me; no more will they call,
Until I've spent all those millions and borrowed some more,
Cause excessive debt is so common and keeps us all poor...

Cruising The Bar After Therapy

A life of peace walked by distressed,
Glancing left to right,
Seeking misplaced comfort
From distressed lives who walked by in peace.

Lives faded in and out
Surrounded by memories of what never was,
Never could be,
And never would be.

She walked on through the agonies and pains confronted,
Heart opening to mind's knowledge.
Relief! Relief! When would it come?

She looked inside
Again,
Hoping and waiting.
She tired of meditating, therapizing, analyzing;
Perhaps it is time to live life.
She'd been observing it so long,
Lost in the analysis, synthesis, and disappointing discoveries.

Damned this search that cries to be followed!
She saw others follow their paths,
Without so many briars and brambles
To scratch and scar them,
Beyond the innocence of younger years,
Yet their paths were not her path.
Arise in me, O Soul that leaves my insides empty.

She sought her soul outside herself,
Where it could never be found:
At the bottom of a tall glass of spirit,
Or rather from that tall glass of water walking by
He did not have it,
But God did he look like he could have!
Arrest him if beauty be illegal.
"Bartender, pour me what's he's having,
And he can have what's left of mine"…

Safety In Strangers

Why do strangers embrace,
Feigning an affection that neither feels,
Trying to replace what once was,
Or what each never found?

All arrived from lonely lives,
Staying in lonely rooms with weary hearts,
Hoping to discover a thrill they missed,
Groping at strangers in illusive expectancy,
Knowing full well the elusive quality
Of the dance.

Why do strangers embrace,
After shunning familiars
Who would embrace them freely and knowingly?

Perhaps there is a safety in strangers,
Who pose no lingering presence,
Who place no probing queries,
And give unconditional affection
More generously than enduring familiars
Seem capable of generating.

Love knows more loneliness
Than any dance of strangers…

Through The Darkness

In the midst of darkness,
I have walked alone,
Sensing the blackness engulf me,
Reaching out in my blindness
To clutch another hand.
There was NONE
To grasp.

Withdrawing my reach,
I stumbled through the darkness
Searching for dim evidence of light,
Clinging to the possibility
That as night gives way to dawn,
The discovery of light
Was inevitable.

Through the darkness,
I walk alone
Sensing the blackness fading,
Straining in my helplessness
To clutch another hand.
There is MINE
To grasp…

Safe Shadows

I used to fear the darkness,
Imagining creatures or giants,
Lurking in the shadows
With harmful intent:
Boyhood images of fright.

I used to wonder
Why I feared the night,
And its accompanying black veil,
Later concluding it was the unknown,
The unseen,
And the un-experienced
That I feared:
Paranoid suspicions of non-existent beings.

Becoming a man, I put those fears away.
I no longer fear the darkness,
Rather I fear the light—
The real creatures and giants
Lurking not in shadows,
But in clear day
With harmful potential:
Manhood images of dread.

I no longer wonder
Why I fear the light,
And its accompanying unveiling,
Concluding it is the known,
The seen,
And the experienced
That I fear:
Accurate realizations of inevitable pain.

For it is in the light
That I face me and others,
Unveiled by the shadows of night,
Unmasked by the black of darkness.

In light, there is no hiding
From past disappointments and irretrievable moments,
Present questions and pressing obligations,
Or future uncertainties and retrospective unfulfillment.

At time, I welcome the darkness,
I once feared.
In the shadows, I am safe
From my own and others' scrutiny,
Being me without confrontation,
Explanation or rationale.
There is no need to hide,
For I am hidden.

In my darkness,
I can choose
What to see,
Know,
And experience.

Some things, I choose not to…

A Child Resides Within Me

A child resides within me,
But…
There is a man around the boy
To listen, nurture, protect
And never abandon the vulnerable child.

My child within is sometimes frightened,
Hurt, lonely, and insecure,
Feeling the eternal pains and needs
Of a childhood that left him scarred.

The man without stands strong with manageable fear,
Healing in solitude and unshakable security,
Feeling the, at times, evasive health
Of a life that helps him grow.

I must listen to the boy's voice,
Once unheeded and often unheard,
For only I, the child's protector
Understands the vulnerabilities,
Fears and needs of the unseen boy.

In the insightful merging
Of the child into the man,
Strength blends with struggle,
Wisdom mixes with curiosity,
And insecurity meets with comfort.

Yes, a child resides within me,
But…
There is a man around the boy,
And, finally,
We are becoming one…

Corners Of Madness

The power of madness frightens me;
Does not matter if it is mine or yours.
No longer do I argue the reality
Of each and everyone being somewhat mad.
My belief stands firm:
Everyone harbors dark, seldom-entered corners
Of frightening madness within,
Where logic and reason cannot enter,
Where destruction and chaos reign supreme,
And fantasies and passion grow beyond control.

I have seen my madness,
And I have cowered in shame.
I have sensed your madness,
And I have shuddered in fear.
We each could destroy ourselves,
And we each could devastate the other.

But… most probably, as those before us,
We will live and die with our madness
Safely tucked away in seldom-entered corners,
Allowing the trusted few to view it,
Keeping the distrusted many far from it…

It Was A Moment Of Irretrievable Times

It was a moment of irretrievable times:
Childhood and the later years flashing scenes,
High speed and too rapid to catch them all.
Choices presented; choices selected.
Paths taken; paths left for later.
Journeys only wondered about, never traveled.

There are moments that change lives,
And all the tomorrows to come
Distance me from the yesterdays,
Sometimes for joy, sometimes for grief.
Bridges span across all these moments
Connecting me to some there that becomes me,
That was me,
That could have been me.

And who I am in this moment,
Expectant with choices
Is life's greatest challenge,
Yesterday's heaviest tear,
Today's purest joy,
And tomorrow's transcendent hope…

Through Brief Darknesses

I noticed one day that I had stopped
Reaching for God and others
To help me through brief darknesses.

Contemplating the next lines,
I ignite another cigarette,
Take a final sip of Chardonnay,
Nibble on a bit of cheddar,
And stare at coffee stains on my desk blotter.

And it occurred to me:
When going through brief darknesses
Some things are easier to hold onto...

Journey Into My Breath Into Me

Breathe in, breathe out,
Faster and deeper,
Close your eyes,
Receive the music
As it maps a path
Across the fissures of your brain.
Light and darkness reside there,
Intertwined like knotted yarn.
Lie still and move… inside,
Deeper inside,
There are spaces that no one knows,
A level where time stands still,
Meanings are unimportant.
Cross over into that spot,
Between sanity and madness.
Linger there in those nether places
Until you, as I, are transported
Backwards or forwards
To times past or times unarrived.
There are moments that change lives,
And you have just re-lived one.
There will be moments that change your life,
And you have just pre-lived another.

Squeeze my hand more tightly;
You must pull me back
When the darkness swallows me.
In the distance are words I understand,
Bringing me back to the room I breathe in,
The bed I lie on.
I have been on a journey
Without time or place,
Distortions of all things I once knew,
Contortions of all I once held true,
And I have no drug in me,
Not recently anyway…

This journey frightens me:
I have entered where I cannot exit,
Slept in a bed from which I cannot arise,
Swam in a turbulent sea,
Drenched still,
Covered with sand and seaweed I cannot brush off,

My brain will not work as before.
Perhaps…
Perhaps that is good, after all;
It's failed me so often.

I took a bite out of a thunderstorm,
And the lightning between my teeth
Electrifies me with stormy power.
I inhaled a blinding sunrise,
And the light inside my mind
Illuminates me with brilliant energy.

"And the Master of Breath formed man
Of the dust of the ground
And breathed into his nostrils
The breath of life
And man became a living soul…"
(Genesis 2:7)

Incubation: Between Shadow And Self

To those who knew him shortly,
He was a man of virtue,
Abiding within the ethics of goodness,
Giving of himself,
Improving the lot of many.

But in the cloak of night-time,
He walked among the shadow people,
Mingling in the darkness.
There are lessons that only the shadows teach,
And one must immerse himself in darkness,
Risk losing, never finding the exit out,
The entrance back into the light.
There are dreams that resemble nightmares,
And nightmares revealing dreams.

A place exists between dark and light,
Between shadow and self,
Where one incubates,
Not yet living, quite distant from death,
Simply waiting to be born,
Moving neither forward nor back:
Nascence of the spirit.
It is so hard to be there,
Groaning with questions,
Awaiting revelations
That no book, no teacher can reveal,
Between dream and nightmare,
Between sleep and awake.

Where he cannot escape,
He ran far and swiftly;
He sought release in her arms,
But they ensnared him,
And he forgot his incubation.
There is a reality that eludes him;
You have seen it, too:
That millisecond of realization,
When it all makes sense somehow.
He held it as water in his hands,
Remaining wet, but empty,
Then dry with no reminder of the water.

Years ago, he was set apart to know,
And he walked away,
Too disconnected to incubate,
But no connexion lasts.
Her eyes can see what he cannot,
Beyond him—other lifetimes.
The sea stretches out endlessly,
The waves relentlessly grasp the earth,
Wanting more than she can give.
Awaken to your purpose here;
Die to your other purpose,
Which only entrap your better dreams.
No relief exists beyond time's passing.

If he knew what was beyond
This incarnation,
He would go there:
Step through the portal that opened
Last night,
He entered her and felt more of his body
Stiffen than just what she encircled.
He could enter her more completely.
Life and death are her powers,
And he awaits both.
How did she learn?
Why did she remember?

My aorta empties page by page,
Blue blood down my arm,
Dripping on this thin sheet;
Clogged arteries distort what once
Came so smoothly.

Go away, not yet;
It's not finished…
He will know when that is true;
And so will you.
There's more to the story,
Than only these glimpses,
Glances of a nether year;
Could be then or now;
No way to know except waiting.

He knew she wanted him,
But he could not respond.
Sand heats up quicker than the water.

Watch my blue blood drip,
And wonder what it all means…

When the madman becomes sane,
He will die,
Or lose all he tried to become.
Insanity makes more sense today;
Virtue also frightened him,
More than the shadows.,
The darkness familiar.
He could touch it more tangibly,
Than he could ever touch her.

Look away,
There is nothing for you here,
Where madness is only one thought away.

What keeps so many striving, so tirelessly:
Those who do not question?
He will never understand you;
There's nothing to relate,
But she will have him tonight,
And never wonder why,
And he will once again forget
What he hurt so hard
To understand…

Those Who Are Supposed To Have The Answers
(or The Paradox of Occupation)

Like a priest who secretly sinned
Yearns for confession and absolution,
Turns to no one in fear of being disrobed,
Cries to his Creator in the darkness of his solitude
And feels so utterly alone.

Like an attorney who committed a heinous crime
Yearns for representation and leniency,
Turns to no one in fear of being disbarred,
Weeps for his Livelihood in the wrongness of his actions
And feels so utterly alone.

Like an artist who cannot create
Yearns for inspiration and masterpieces,
Turns to no one in fear of being discovered,
Cries to his Spirit in the bleakness of his talent
And feels so utterly alone.

So the psychologist who is secretly insane
Yearns for understanding and direction,
Turns to no one in fear of seeming demented,
Cries for his Condition in the irony of his insanity
And alone so utterly feels.

Perhaps only sinful priests can forgive,
Who after wrestling with their own sins
Finally understand a guilty soul's desperation for absolution

Perhaps only attorneys who cross illicit lines can represent,
Who once immersed in defending their own lives in the system,
Finally comprehend the fear of clients,
The price of justice, and the relief of acquittal.

Perhaps only doubting artists can finally create,
Who obsess about the perfect color or canvass or word or rhyme,
Afraid to begin, though finally and confidently,
They create many imperfect masterpieces, full of doubt and wonder.

And perhaps only troubled psychologists can understand,
Who earned their compassion from their own childhood violations,
And acquired their healing from adulthood edification, focus and perseverance,
Finally wise enough to know that "the answers" are a process,
And many scars in life will only fade, but never be undone…

Come Walk With Me Through My House Of Pain

Come walk with me through my house of pain:
Enter in this corridor of masks,
Stroll the hallway filled with pictures
Of people I have been,
Sit in my living room of the mundane,
Dine in the kitchen of my creativity,
Descend with me into the cellar of my darkest secrets,
Ascend with me into the attic,
Of the treasured, past moments of my life,
Explore these closets in due time,
When you have earned my trust
To display my embarrassing disarray.

And so it was, as such, for years
I was escorted by the curious, the desperate,
The brave and the reincarnated lonely ones
Through their internal homes,
Allowed to tour and linger
In worlds where even the most trusted
Often and usually remain uninvited.

And these daily tours
Sent me deep within,
Deep within the architecture
Of my own internal home.
It was not a tour I wished to avoid,
Simply one I did not wish
To take with such daily frequency...

The Lock Is On The Inside

Belonging feelings come and go:
At times connected and meaningfully relating
To a mystical and scary extent;
At times so disconnected and alone,
That it seemed no one could penetrate my darkness.

I have constructed and escaped from
Innumerable emotional walls and prisons.
Some were built of foggy, yet transparent glass.
I vaguely saw others;
They vaguely saw me,
Authentic hearing and touching obstructed.
Other walls I build of solid brick and mortar
With all external sight, sound, and contact prevented.
No one entered;
I did not exit.

I have watched others construct their walls,
Knocked against their glass,
And chiseled at their mortar,
Trying to expose a hand-sized opening
To reach through
To their self-constructed, lonely prison,
And hand them a mirror and a key,
So they may see themselves,
And indisputably know
That the lock is on the inside...

Our Canvasses Speak Without Words

Sitting in quiet repose,
Gazing at blank canvas,
Mixing fresh paints,
Imagining vivid pictures:
Ocean waves and distant seagulls,
Mountain tops and river rapids,
And ancient castles and wandering fairies;
She begins.

No one ever really taught her
To paint what she sees inside.
A few did guide her to create
New pictures and different color mixtures,
But no one could ever teach her
What she already knows:
To paint.

She does not paint because she likes to;
She paints because she has to,
Which is the only true mark of an artist.
She creates because she has no choice,
Desiring inner harmony and peace.

Sitting in quiet solitude,
Gazing at blank canvas,
She is free
To release her binding fears,
Express her nurturing love,
Create her own smiling world,
And share her inspiring spirit.

Though she never told me,
From her I have learned:
Life is but a blank canvas.
Throughout our journey, we are handed
Assortments of paints, brushes, and choices,
And in the end
Our canvasses speak without words:
Either brilliant and full of light;
Drab, void of color and unfinished;
Or abstract messes and misunderstood.
And... we can begin again!
She begins...

Loneliness Rides The Streets Tonight

Loneliness rides the streets tonight:
Endless streams of redundant beams,
Bright white in front,
Dim red eyes in the rearview,
Loner insomniacs searching for the elusive,
Listening to overly cool DJ's on the F.M.,
Feeling moist, cool air in the a.m.

Who's in the coupe that just passed,
Or the sedan on my tail?
Perhaps a second shift nurse,
Finally going home as she ponders
The aged man in Room 109 who may not see the dawn,
And wonders at the sincerity of the young physician's proposition.
Perhaps a third shift orderly,
Headed to another unfulfilling night of work,
Wondering how he can afford
Those earrings his wife wants
For her birthday next month,
And wondering why he dropped out
To say, "I do" so prematurely.
Maybe a middle-aged man
Enjoying not answering to her anymore,
As to his where's and who-with's,
But still feeling the pain of a lonely bed
And a too-small, unfamiliar apartment.

Yes, loneliness rides the streets tonight,
And I ride along,
Pondering purposes and meanings,
Glancing at the red and white parade
In search of the elusive…

Giving Up The Meaning Struggle

Night sounds push against my locked windows,
While stillness and solitude beckon me,
Sitting alone, wordless thoughts,
Endlessly racing in and out of cerebral chambers.

I struggle for meaning and find none;
Not one that convinces me
That endless sleep would not be my salvation.
All things I desire elude me,
Like some lone deer racing in and out
Of trees and thickets, hiding and being hidden,
Pursued by a cold, hungry hunter
Who fired his last ammunition at a squirrel,
And missed…
I am the hunter, the hopeless pursuer.

Daylight peeps between my curtained windows,
While activity and intimacy frighten me;
Writing alone with thoughtless words
Temporarily pouring out of aortal chambers.

I struggle for nothing and find meaning…

That Big Piece Of Canvas

I stood in that museum,
Mesmerized by your talent,
Larger than life,
Stroked like birth trauma
With tears and perfect colors.

"You did it," I said silently,
Hoping somewhere in time,
You could hear me,
As I gazed at that large painting,
Remembering that summer day,
Months ago when we drove away
From that art supply store,
Where you bought the largest canvas
You could find,
And cried with tears of doubt,
As we drove away in summer heat,
The convertible's top down.
You held the canvas from flying out
Of the windy car,
Questioning yourself.
I stumbled, but tried to remind you
Who you are.

Now, here I stand before that big piece of canvas,
Brilliantly, perfectly created,
In this museum, and the only creation
That stops these people in their tracks,
Hypnotized by its perfection,
Stunned by its uniqueness,
Is yours.
And to think, it could have blown away,
Right out of that car
On that warm, tearful summer day.

I am glad you held it tightly,
And inspired that you converted
An artist's doubt and a poet's tears
Into heavenly colors as you released your fears.

I knew you could from the start;
Grateful you re-discovered your art…

Drop-In Clinic For The Lonely

The ebony lady removes her top,
As the bearded, drunken man
Talks sincerely to someone
That none of us can see.

To whom does he speak and why?
Perhaps an old war buddy,
Who never returned home with him;
Perhaps the wife from his younger years,
Who took the kids when she took the house;
Perhaps to his teenage sweetheart,
Who left his arms, but never left his heart;
Perhaps to the son he fathered a decade ago,
Whom he abandoned from confusion and fear.
Perhaps he talks to no one.
Maybe he only listens to the voices
That will not be drowned
In two or even twenty Bloody Marys.

The ebony lady continues dancing,
Exposed body grinding sensuously
To the pulsating beat
To songs that the bearded man cannot hear.

He would not notice her if
She had three breasts and two navels,
But if he would quit talking to his unseen friends,
And flailing his hands around him,
I would not be so distracted
In my enjoyment of the ebony lady,
Swaying to the sensuous music,
In this drop-in clinic for the lonely…

Visits With The Father

There he sat at the middle of the bar
With four-year-old son, Tommy,
The Wednesday evening visiting father
Telling stories to an eager boy
About "what we'll do this weekend,"
Promises to replace the absence.
A fatherless family in a fragmented void,
Straining to fill roles
For which none have models.

I pictured the father taking Tommy home,
Back to his mother and the house he once shared,
Hugging Tommy tightly in the car,
Assuring him of the fun to happen this weekend.
Sitting in his idling car,
As Tommy runs toward the front door,
And the flying moth-encircled porch light,
Ringing the doorbell
Looking back at his father in the car.

Tommy waves a hand,
As his mother opens the door;
Straining his gaze to see his father
Through darkened car windows;
The door closes as father slowly backs out
Of the once-familiar driveway,
And he drives away in grieving silence,
Telling stories to his aching heart
About "what we'll do this weekend…"

Ode To The Bartender

Bottles and bottles line the shelves,
Filled with illusions and dreams—
Never imagined, never dreamt;
Perhaps once imagined, perhaps once dreamt;
Contained,
Until they're poured
Into the glasses and mugs
Of those who lost their visions,
Of those who lost their dreams;
Those who lost their way...

They consume the concocted mixtures
In quiet desperation of rejuvenation;
Abandoned dreams, abandoned imaginings;
Abandoned lives, abandoned realities.
There are no dailies here;
Simply revived pursuit of the fantasies
Which ran rampant in the naiveté of youth.
How they yearn for those fantasies,
Once imagined, forever remembered.

You, dear bartender, serve important magic,
If only temporary and illusive,
For you pour the elixir of fantasies
And, if only but for a moment,
You return the dreams to dull lives...

Two Men At The Bar

They sit across the empty bar,
Talking of golf scores and the World Series,
Endless stories of missed strokes and stolen bases;
Strangers in a familiar bar,
Hiding behind cigar smoke and vodka tonics,
Silently wondering if their wives care
That they are late to home once again.

It is connection they seek here,
Dreading the decades of disconnection at home,
Missing their grown children,
They work overtime to educate;
Wondering if they will come home this semester for the holidays,
Wishing they had the chance again
To teach their sons the lessons they have only recently learned.

One man rises to settle his tab,
As the other checks his watch, fingers his empty glass,
And wonders if she's asleep yet at home.
Both men leave, shaking hands at the door,
Separating to their individual cars and contemplative silences,
Later tiptoeing through darkened houses
To quietly lie down beside sleeping, distant wives,
And stare sleeplessly at separate, dimly-lit ceilings…

In A Man's World

In a man's world:
There are Longings to be known by woman and man,
And there is Sadness that being known may never occur.
There are Fathers who handed down a legacy of Silence,
Who then died before breaking the Silence to reveal the mysteries.
There are Fathers whom he has never met,
And present Fathers who were heroes, yet strangers.

In a man's world:
There are Mothers who birthed him and loved him;
And there are Mothers who tolerated, then ignored him.
There are Sons and Daughters who worship him,
And there are Sons and Daughters who wonder who he is.
There are Brothers with whom he competes, yet caretakes,
There are Brothers for whom he would give his life,
And there are Brothers to whom for years he has remained silent.

In a man's world:
There are silent Fears and determined Ambitions,
And there are ancient Scars and secret Yearnings.
There are Fantasies of sailing uncharted Seas,
Discovering Treasures, and enchanting unmet Princesses.
There is Pride in doing and Confusion in being,
And there is Security in having and Shame in losing.
There are Demons whose names he knows
And there is Darkness whose depths he fears.

In a man's world:
There are Mentors whom he admires and to whom he listens,
And there are Mentors with whom he competes, then leaves.
There is a little Boy inside who loves to laugh and play,
And there is a powerful Man outside protecting the internal Boy.
There is a Woman whom he loves, but cannot tell;
And there is a Woman whom he despises, but says he loves.
There are other Men whom he loves, but fears to tell,
And Men who frighten him because they are such a mirror.
There are Men who give up and secretly take their own lives,
And there are Men who die slowly, piece by grieving piece.

In a man's world:
There is much to Love and much to Fear;
There is much to Enjoy and much to Sadden;
There is much to Admire and much to Question;
And much to Understand and much to Confuse.

Last night, I met an old friend for dinner.
He offered his hand to shake…
Instead, with trepidation, I embraced him:
Male energy strengthened by male energy;
For I knew he understood me
Because he is a Man…

In A Woman's World

I have wondered what it is like to be you:
You have an opening,
Where I have an appendage.
You can grow life inside you;
I can only watch, amazed, from the outside.
Your breasts protrude smooth, filled with fatty tissue;
My chest expands, hairy and muscular.

You can speak lewdly to me,
And I might feel flattered.
I speak lewdly to you,
And I might be slapped.
You could fondle a strange man in public,
And he could be aroused.
I could fondle you in our first meeting,
And you would feel assaulted;
I could be arrested.

You can wear clothes like me,
And be called professional.
I could wear clothes like you,
But be called perverted.
You could display mannerisms like me,
And be called strong and aggressive.
I could display mannerisms like you,
And be called weak and even worse.

This seems unfair, Woman,
That you can be like me,
But I cannot be like you.
No wonder I want to penetrate you.
How does it feel to be you…
Inside?!…

Connecting The Dots

Draw a straight line from one to two,
Three to four to five, on and on,
Not so difficult, then the numbers get bigger,
More crowded with unexpected curves,
Until only a few numbers remain.
Then, I sat back, dropped my pencil
And smiled at the elephant that emerged,
When before, I saw only a page
Of numbered dots and an occasional stray line;
Just a boy connecting the dots, completing pictures.

Now an adult, whose life occasionally
Resembles a page of numbered dots and stray lines,
And I have no idea what the finished picture will be.
Easiest in the beginning and end,
But here I am stuck in the middle,
Trying to find the next number, the next step.
Which path shall I choose?
How many more numbers
Until I've completed the picture?

I suppose one day I'll sit back,
Drop my pencil and smile
At the completed picture,
Content with what emerged
From this page, my life,
But for now,
I am hovering on number 30;
Where the hell's that 31?...

Driving Slowly By The Middle Years

One day I noticed
While driving
That I braked and slowed
As children walked beside the road
And I cautiously drove by
As elders of this land
Crossed the streets with cane in hand.

I never slowed, you see,
For the middle-aged morning runners
Or young couples taking honeymoon walks,
Nor even for the business talks
Of the ambitious 35-year-olds
Crossing the streets
From his office to lunch café.

One day I noticed
While driving
That somewhere along the way,
I had stopped celebrating
The middle of life,
Seeing only the beginning innocent years
And the ending wisdom years
As precious enough to slow me down
To notice.

These are the middle years:
Far removed from the playgrounds
Of my past,
Yet distant still from the trembling wisdom
Of my future.

So much responsibility to address;
So many working hours to labor;
So many necessities to acquire;
So many luxuries to desire.

Far from the cradle, I know,
Far from the casket, I hope,
Sometime between the playgrounds
And the wrinkles, I think.

These are the middle years:
The days I silently longed for
From the prison of playgrounds,
The days I will fondly recall
From the future winter days of my life.

These are the middle years:
The days I choose
To remember,
To celebrate,
To slow down,
To notice…

The Abandonment Of Silence

Sitting in silent wonder,
She watched him with awe,
Delighting in his wisdom,
Bathing in her curiosity.
Mysteries revealed;
Secrets still concealed.

They talked for hours
With their hearts and souls,
Dripping revelation from their tongues
Like thick raindrops falling
On parched, barren land;
He absorbed her intriguing words.
She bathed in his unique ideas.

Through the early afternoon,
Into the windy, dusky,
Then darkened evening,
They spoke of life and love,
Of gods and spirits, of pain and beauty;
Holding hands with their pasts;
Reaching forward into their futures;
As they each vulnerably abandoned
The sadness and distrust of silence...

The Devastation Of Betrayal

Into the sacred depths of his path,
They tread with vows of respect:
That no matter the twists and turns,
Betrayal would not be shown,
Walked with him through midnights and sunrises,
Then that most dreaded bend in their road arrived,
And they could venture not one more step.

The sun rose at midnight yesterday,
And stars shone brightly at mid-day;
Altered state, altered time;
Consciousness prevails, though strains to rhyme.

Laughter resounds through the travails of pain,
Like mystical lightning shatters the clouds of rain
On stormy days, hibernating sun, caves of clouds;
Lost in meaningless searches for the meaningful.
Where black is not dark, and white is color,
He wandered on beyond that dreaded bend,
Believing he could transcend solitude,
Disown vengeful fantasies, intricately plotted,
Infinitely planned... not implemented,
Fearing reciprocal karma,
Knowing the universe always rights itself.
It needs not his help.

Their day would arrive...

I'll Come To You

Enter too soon,
Scare me away.
Wait in the shadows,
Maybe I'll stay.

Enter me softly,
So much to hide.
Question me gently,
Or I will not confide.

Come into my world,
Slowly at first.
Please keep your distance,
My answers are rehearsed.

Enter too soon,
Scare me away.
Wait in the shadows,
Or I've nothing to say…

A Life In The Day Of Calvin

If drugs are a way to access unexplored brain places,
Then Calvin has tapped into more consciousness than anyone I know.
Fifteen years of needles and snorts and hooters and shooters
And capsules and trips and 'shrooms and anything else
He could find… to immunize himself
From too much continuous unaltered reality.
I listened to him complain about planetary destruction,
Political hypocrisy, materialist snobs, unaware middle-classers,
And the way everyone's priorities were all whacked out, man.

He did another water bong,
Said he feels so much better since
He stopped smoking cigarettes three years ago,
Says he wished be had stayed in college,
Had to sell his nine-year-old truck, couldn't afford it,
Wonders why his relationships don't last very long,
And thinks he doesn't call his parents as much as he should.

Water bong bubbles again: another hooter.

His lethargic, yet ever hopeful house dog drops a worn tennis ball in Calvin's lap.
He holds in the water-filtered weed, tells the Labrador to, "Go away,"
And asks me for the third time,
"Do you really think the pawn shop will go fifteen bucks on that old stereo?
Then I could get some beer for the weekend."

I listened to him complain about planetary destruction,
Political hypocrisy, materialist snobs, unaware middle-classers,
And the way everyone's priorities are all whacked-out, man.
Everyone's priorities all whacked-out, man.
Priorities all whacked-out, man.
All whacked-out man…
Man!
Whacked-out man!

So Calvin accessed unexplored brain places,
And slowly self-destructs
In the expansion of consciousness…

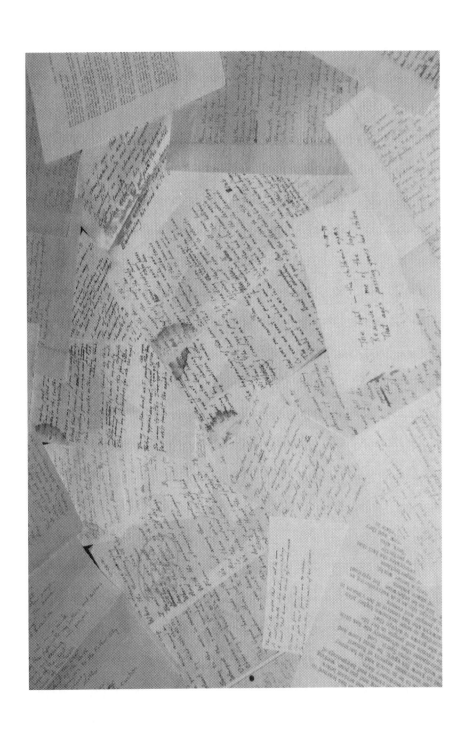

A Poet And A Napkin

The napkin poet arises in me,
Bidding me, bleed my pen,
To create the truths I strain to believe,
On some unsuspecting napkin, I long to relieve.

Release my mind from its overflow of words,
Words that crowd my restless spirit,
Requesting freedom, escape now through my ink;
Etch your truths on this napkin; make me think.

But not too much thought as this day ends,
In the arranging of words, my sanity depends,
Bleeding my pen on this fabric of white,
Etching my philosophies far into the night.

Bring another drink as I ponder this verse;
Poetry appears my sweet eternal curse.
So many truths, I cannot clearly see,
Yet still tonight, the napkin poet arises in me...

Concert In The Winter Of Her Fifteenth Year

She remembered the winter of her fifteenth year;
Winter concert one evening after school;
Cafeteria converted to a parent-filled orchestra hall;
Schedule included her original score written only weeks ago.

Practicing days and sleepless nights preceded her performance;
Determined to flawlessly strike those ivory and ebony keys;
Reveal her melodic creation to all who stilled to listen;
She would play for them what she alone heard in her heart.

Then, the evening arrived with anxiety and anticipation;
An eternal hour passed before her revealing solo performance;
Then, she flawlessly unveiled her heart's private tune;
Arising to applause from the piano, with unseen tears of pride.

There are moments that change lives:
Moments filled with magic and meaning;
Moments never forgotten; events crystal clear always;
That winter evening in her fifteenth year was one such moment...

Holly-Day Twenty-One

Twenty-one years of life now seen:
Joys and pains, and all the in-betweens;
The road ahead, so wide open to you,
So much yet to experience; so much yet to view.

Life's hallways will present to you many doors,
Gothic ceilings above you, brilliantly marble-tiled floors;
Houses filled with opportunities await people like you,
Inviting and welcoming ANYTHING you might choose to do!

Such beauty you've attained in this woman I see,
And your heart, kind and gentle, has deeply touched me.
The smiles that you give can melt me inside,
And your sensuous ways cannot be denied.

You listen so well as someone spills out their soul,
Offering compassion when friends' lives are out of control.
So, many perceptive people adore the lady you have become;
Life's unpleasantries have not made your giving heart numb.

Thus, my special friend, these twenty-one lines is my gift to you.
Never forget the best sage's wisdom: To thine own self, be true.
And remember that all roads you might choose, a price you will pay.
I am grateful to know you on this, your most special Holly-day;
May the very best of life, bliss, and dreams always come your way!

A Confessional Booth

Stepping inside,
The door closed behind her.
She said her last time here
Was long ago,
Told him where she wanted to be,
Then began confessing her sins
One by one.

Silently, the 'priest' listened
As she cried
Words of pain
Until she fell silent.
All her sins remembered;
All her sins revealed.
Compassionately then he spoke
Words of comfort,
Gave suggestions
Which might be useful,
And assured her that others also
Have sinned as such,
Many far greater than she.

Silence again between them
In the confessional booth.
Contemplatively, she sat relieved,
Unburdened by her past,
Grateful to not know this 'priest',
Grateful for the darkness concealment,
Grateful that she would never see him again,
Forgiving herself enhanced
By his non-judgment.

She began gathering her things together,
Less troubled, preparing
To shamelessly step outside,
As they both arrived
At her intended destination
In his taxi…

A Toast To The Muse

Disinhibiting Liquid: Release what you cannot control:
    Those lines that burn within my soul:
      Words to charm, words to amuse;
      Words to alarm, words to confuse.

    I toast the Muse, on this verseful night,
      For on my spirit, she shines her light.
      Guide my pen as it records
    What my heart bleeds, but cannot afford.

    I have followed you now for many years,
      Through times of joy, and more of tears.
These rhymes my passion; verses about my life,
    Through all the happiness, all the strife.

    Words in darkness seeking the light;
    Visions of a blind man yearning for sight.
I pay them this flowing tribute for being my gift:
    My footsteps, they guide; my spirit, they lift.

    One could do worse than poetically be.
    With rhyming eyes, this world I see,
    Until death do we part, this gift will I use
To bring light to my darkness; and gain what I lose…

The Indecision Of Change

So then, life changes again,
And grief and joy, the companions
Of changes unexpected and uncertain.
I cannot stay; I cannot go,
Yet I must do either.
Both cannot co-exist.

I cannot leave you here,
Nor am I prepared to take you there.
Damn these miles that separate
What I must do from what I want.
Yet, what I want is here,
And what I want is there.
Damn this body that confines my spirit
To one place, one path!

Thus, Frost understood long ago:
Only one road, one traveler could he be,
Not two, and certainly not three.
I would take you there,
But it is not time...
All so difficult this is,
Just as those lines refusing to rhyme...

Four Days And Two Weeks

Looking back I now realize
How special the then commonplace is.
I watched you play in the evenings,
Held you as you cried over a toddler's pains,
Listened while you splashed bath water,
Singing happily songs only you knew.
I read you stories and listened to prayers at bedtime,
Thanking your mystical God for your family,
Picked you up from daycare, then preschool.
I was there for many of your moments.

Looking back I now realize
How I wish I had firmly grasped each moment,
Now seeing how tenuous such moments can be.

Now I call you on the phone,
Listening to your excited, sad voice,
And die a little inside, as we grunt simulated hugs,
And blow unseen kisses that distance prevents giving and feeling.
You show me your half-healed wounds made in my absence,
Unavailable to hold your tears tightly.
I hear your splashes in an alternate weekend tub,
Wishing your songs were as happily sung as before.

Four nights each month and two weeks each summer,
I place the stuffed animals by your head,
Read you stories and wonder what you mean
As you thank your mystical God for your family.
I am absent for many of your moments;
You learned to tie your shoes without me.

I was your daily Daddy;
Now an infrequent, confusing non-custodial father
Who still yearns to share your daily moments.
I want to see your apprehension and shy face
That first day of kindergarten;
To plot your growth year by year on a priceless wall-chart;
To see you first ride an unsteady bicycle,
And hold you if you wreck on an unkind pavement.
I want to witness your creative mind develop,
Hear about your grade school scrapes and girlfriends,
And urge you daily to study and play hard.
To hear your little boy's voice crackle the first time

As you shed the skin of boyhood.
I want to watch you be a child and become a man,
And give you those parts of me worth giving,
Traits unlikely to be adopted during
Four days each month and two weeks of summer.

Last week you said good-bye… hanging up the phone
Without the tears or hesitance of prior calls.
Today when I came to your preschool,
We walked hands-clasped through the grass
While I felt you feeling awkward and unfamiliar,
And as we sat to talk of grass and yellow flowers,
Your eyes did not look at mine.
I wondered if you did not want to feel close to me,
Distancing yourself, awaiting the redundant lines:
"I love you and I'll see you in a few days."
"I love you , but I must go."
It's sad to see a son protect himself
From the pain of a father's absence.
I shall still wonder when you pray at bedtime
To your mystical God:
"Thank you for my family…"

A Thousand Miles Away

Called my son tonight,
A thousand miles away,
To hear about his first school day.
After two busy-signal attempts,
She...
Answered...
Said he was asleep early,
After an exciting kindergarten day.
Following two insistences on my part,
And hateful reluctance on her part,
She awakened my kindergarten-tired, sleeping son.

He groggily answered the phone
And fell asleep before we finished.
Gone were the excitement and stories
Of his first school day;
Left was a lethargic, sleepy voice
Only saying, "It was good."

Another missed moment in his life.
Missed his anticipation and anxious eyes,
Missed snapping the historical first-day-of-school picture,
Meeting Ms. Whoever and seeing his classroom,
Hearing about new friends, Billy and Bobby,
And the kid in second row who cried all day,
Then went home early,
Missed seeing his colored pictures
With purple trees and yellow skies,
And missed his excitely telling his discoveries
Of recess, big pencils, monkey bars, and school playgrounds.

This is the price I pay:
His mother, no longer my wife,
Court-decided custodian of my son,
Who has a telephone father
Hurtfully missing his many fleeting moments
A thousand miles away...

"One Time..." Stories

On your seventh birthday,
I came to visit
Bringing the jeans you needed,
The wallet you wanted,
And a size 4 initial ring,
Colorfully wrapped and red-ribboned.

A piece of cake was saved for me
From the party I had missed
Which I ate with you at the table,
Beneath the balloons I never blew up.
In the living room lay torn wrapping paper
And previously-opened birthday gifts and cards.

Your mother loaned her bicycle.
I followed you on yours to the park,
Where my child inside played
On slides, swings, and bars
With the child you are.
I listened to your "One time..." stories:
"One time I got a splinter in my finger...
One time we buried a boy in the sand...
One time these kids killed a snake with rocks...
One time..."

As our swings went back and forth,
You said, "I come here sometimes
To play while Mommy works inside,"
Pointing to the clubhouse nearby.
"Grandpa and Grandma don't always want to watch me,
Cause I'm always having lots of energy,
And they get tired."
I laughed and said,
"It's neat that you have lots of energy,"
Hoping to affirm your childhood zeal.
"Yeah, I know," you responded.
"They're just getting old."

You picked up a stick,
Transformed it into a cane,
Tried to talk with a shaky voice,
Laughingly pretending to be old.
I borrowed the stick-cane,

Spoke with a grin and a shaky old voice,
Pretended to lean on a giggling you, as we walked,
And fleetingly pondered the years ahead.

I watched you with paternal delight,
Played with you in child-like freedom,
And thought of when I will indeed be old
Hoping that someday, you will remember
And still be telling "One time..." stories:
"One time on my seventh birthday, my Dad and I..."

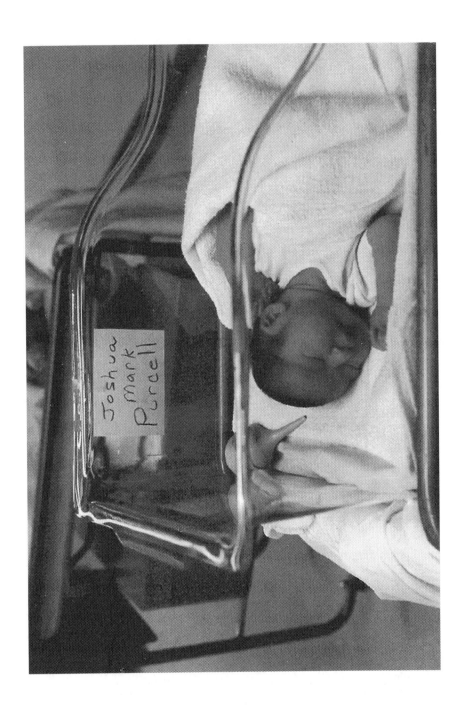

I Stood At The Window

I stood at the window,
Watched the loading ramp withdraw,
The jet back away,
Then taxi toward the runway.
Moving to a different window,
Waving to his unseen face
Wondering if he could see me.

I stood at the window,
Watching the airplane gain momentum
Until it lifted into the wind,
Taking you... again
Far away from me.
I stood at the window,
Watching as it grew smaller and smaller
Until even the remaining speck of him
Eluded my sight.

I stood at the window,
A visiting father missing him, my son,
Whose tears still dampened my shoulder,
Whose departing weeping face haunted me,
The end of another school holiday visit
With all the sadness that separating delivers.

Eleven years ago when he arrived,
I had no idea that life would change so.
I wept joyfully at his newness,
Loving everything about who he would become,
Reading the name label on his crib,
Connecting him to me from where
I stood at the window...

There is no joy in parting...

Sixteen Years With My Son

Sixteen candles upon your birthday cake;
Blow them out, Son, as a wish you make.
Enjoy this day; enjoy the coming years.
May you always have hope and a shortage of fears.

No longer a boy, Son, and becoming a man.
Always speak truth and be as kind as you can.
Listen to others in caring and helpful ways.
You'll need them sometimes, too, on your own cloudy days.

You're a beautiful person, my Son, you are!
With a likable personality that will carry you far;
And your humor: contagious with that magical smile.
How often I miss you; wish we could visit awhile.

Sixteen years since I first saw your face.
You entered this world and in my life took your place.
So many great moments and memories we have had;
So many reasons I always feel proud when you call me Dad…

Along The Creek Banks Of Childhood

There are days when the trees that grew
Along the creek banks of my childhood
Appear vividly in my mind,
And I am young once again, walking
With our family shepherd and a boy's stick
Beside that creek as the sun glistens,
With blinding brilliance off the gently flowing waters;
Fully alive with immortal years of some mystical future,
Savoring all the naïve innocence that youthfulness contains,
Believing that tomorrow's bottle will release my genie;
Granting all the wishes that a boy may dream,
Walking beside a glistening creek beneath those trees.

But youth passes, fading more quickly than summer's
Green leaves becoming autumn's multi-colored spectacle,
And the sun can hide behind clouds
Pregnant with rain falling in gentle creeks,
Swelling up and out beyond the water's banks;
And innocence once savored is swept away
Beneath life's dark and rushing waters,
And that genie's bottle of tomorrow's wishes
Becomes cracked and tarnished, sometimes lost
Within the yesterdays of detours and dead end streets.

But... there are still those days,
When the trees that grew
Along the banks of my childhood
Appear vividly in my heart,
Reminding me...
And I am young...once again...

Late Night Contemplations

Once again it is past midnight,
As I sit alone and contemplate.
All others in my brother's house asleep.
There is a freedom in the night-time,
When all but convenient stores are closed;
Television is too boring to leave on,
And work demands will wait till morning.

With the darkness pressing against the windows,
And the headlights from the few remaining street roamers
Brighten, then dim past the curtains,
I sit and enjoy my solitude—
Contemplating goals and dreams,
Severed relationships and present romance;
Lives I might live and those I have,
And my own life's brevity and mortality
Startle me!

It's time to burst forth from the starting post;
I've been waiting in the gate too long,
Ever wondering how the race will develop:
Imagining, strategizing, and assuming…
I must objectify my goals,
Awaken my slumbering dreams,
Release the past and embrace the present,
Live my life and build on the lived foundation,
Regain my faith that
My life's quality translates its quantity,
And realized dreams
Make one's life Immortal…

A Teacher Completed The Circle

This morning, a teacher completed the circle,
Crossing over into the land of rising suns,
Eternal spirit exiting her aged body,
Leaving behind her tired and weary mind.

Her mate nurtured the earth and her creatures;
Over fifty years together, growing corn and birthing calves,
Caring for their children, and loving their grandchildren,
Watching o'er the land, harvesting all that She produced.

For nearly four decades, her garden was the classroom;
For nearly forty years, her flowers were our children.
She fed the hungry minds of countless little ones;
She watched over the children of a thousand parents.

For most of her life, she planted the wheat of wisdom,
Sowed the corn of ambition, and the seeds of dreams
In the hearts and minds of hundreds of students;
She is leaving behind a legacy of learning.

We knew her as Teacher;
We knew her as Mother;
We knew her as Grandmother,
Who taught us history,
And shaped our futures…

The Green, Porch Swing

As a boy he remembers visiting their house,
Always looking forward to sitting in the green, porch swing.
In the earliest memories, his tiny legs stuck straight out,
Too short for knees to bend over the edge
While Grandpa or Grandma, sometimes both,
Pushed their feet against the wooden porch floor,
Moving the swing slowly and calmly back and forth.

His little-boy legs grew and soon, sitting on the swing's edge
With tip-toes, he could push against the floor,
Smiling a little-boy smile as the swing moved, though jerky and uneven.

In time, the little boy became a teenager
With longer legs than Grandpa or Grandma.
When he visited, they still sat in the green, porch swing,
While his feet pushed the floor, moving the swing
As he had learned: slowly and calmly, back and forth,
And he listened to their stories of yesterday:
How they moved north and worked long days for only a few cents an hour,
Yet had all they needed and much they wanted.
He learned of his mother's childhood escapades,
And saw pictures of relatives he had never met and never could meet.
Grandpa told him of driving the ice cream truck
Through the town which was now a lake with weekend boating,
And about his only ticket when the speed limit was thirty-five.
On the green, porch swing, they watched the busy traffic,
And talked of fatalities and dust since the new road came through.
The boy remembered when trees and houses
Stood peaceful and quiet where the cars now drove.
In the swing, he drank gallons of the best iced-tea,
As Grandma never let his glass get too empty.

Years have quickly passed with a speed they both predicted,
And the boy is now a man.
The little boy in him often remembers the many stories
Heard in the green, porch swing:
He heard about kindness and giving and honesty;
He learned that things change and people adjust and go on;
He discovered the importance of family and God;
And he always felt their generous love and admiration.
More important than any story told or lesson learned
From Grandpa and Grandma, the most special gift
Was knowing that he was valued and precious enough

For them to take time to swing calmly, slowly, and lovingly,
Back and forth with him in the green, porch swing.

As life gets busier and years pass more quickly by,
Times are needed to find comfort and peace
In the boyhood memories of yesterday.
Such are the memories of Grandpa, Grandma,
And me: the little boy in the green, porch swing…

The Light In Her Living Room Window

The light in her living room window is always on,
    As she sits alone in the house they shared.
She has lived long enough to see her daughter retire,
    And for her grandsons to be middle-aged men.
Even most of her fourth generation are now adults.
Her God once more blessed her life with enough time
    To see her fifth generation walking about.

She remains the quite, humble matriarch
Of a family scarred by struggles, but surrounded by success.
There is a goodness in her family passed on
By her and her late life mate to her precious daughter
Who passed the baton forward to her own two sons.
They carried the thread of goodness forward still
To their children and her great, great grandchildren.

She is the daughter of a young woman
Who ventured to town one day and received a free ride
On a merry-go-round, who said she never got off,
From an older, handsome man who teased
That his S.S. name stood for SunShine.

She is the granddaughter of a Union soldier
Who fought in the Civil War for the winning North
Who still found time to father twenty-two children
One of those: her father who gave a special young woman
A special free ride on a carousel one day in the center of town.
Her father drove geese, cobbled shoes, and kept his seventeen children
And half the neighbors well-fed during that Great Depression.

Her beloved husband went on nearly twenty years ago,
    Crossing over, preparing for her to arrive some year.
He visits now with her grandparents, parents, sister, brothers
And many friends, healed and whole, in harmony in paradise.
    Someday on the other side, after she goes there,
He will introduce her to the son she carried, but never knew,
Who departed her world the same painful day he was born.

She sits in their home, missing her husband's presence
    Every day since he slipped away from her.
    Some days she aches to see him again,
But she can wait, smiling with memories, enjoying watching
    Several generations growing, building their lives,

As my grandmother, the daughter of SunShine
Sits beside the light,
Always on in her living room window:
Just like the light of her loving influence,
Always on and shining like a beacon inside each of us,
Reminding us of family and where we came from,
And to never underestimate how far into the future
A free carousel ride can reach…

Dancing Across Black And White Keys

My mother singing in her room,
Some medley of verses from yesterdays, from years ago,
Starting and stopping, at times in mid-verse, mid-word,
Returning to the first line again, perfecting the tune,
Or perfecting the playfulness of some silly song.
"Let the merry sunshine in. Let the merry sunshine in.
Open all your windows. Open all your doors.
Let the merry sunshine in."
Some tunes reaching back to her own kindergarten years.

My mother was often singing in some other room,
As my life began, as life shaped me, molding me.
Her melodies and piano-caressing served me, nurtured me,
As some reliable and soothing soundtrack to the ever-changing unfolding of my life,
No doubt cultivating the creative within me, singing a dormant poet awake,
Instilling hope and gentleness, melody and laughter in my brother and me.

Sitting in her home, I hear her now, busying herself
With organizing tasks in the next room, now audibly,
Then quietly singing her verses, as she moves about.
Often, I know the tunes, could even sing along with her;
Sometimes she slips back more years than I am, and sings along
With some radio tune from a 1951 Ford that I never rode inside.
I can see my father smile at her as he drives along, arm around her, listening,
Enjoying her songs, young and in love, admiring his new singing Juliet.

My mother singing in her room, replaying pieces of her own life:
The joys, the pleasures; the grief, the pain; memories before me and after me;
Songs that trigger my own reflections, replaying pieces of my own life;
Comforting me with black and white keys and her melodic voice that has
Warmed me over four decades now, vividly coloring the memories of years long
gone.

When I am away, off on my own life's adventures and unfolding,
It is her music and singing that I miss so much;
There is no sound sweeter than a mother's melodies
Sang with love and laughter to the innocent heart of her child.
I can see my brother and me then, and I see our children now,
Smiling and listening, laughing and singing along, always admiring,
As her enchanting voice floats across notes and lyrics,
As the hands of our mother dance across black and white keys,
Giving her gift of music to the soundtracks of our lives...

115

Voice Tone Of Silk In The Key Of Magic

Lyrics dripped from her throat like long awaited raindrops,
Falling on us: desert-barren flowers, thirsty and blossoming,
As her sound pierced and consoled our hearts, wounded and injured
With the lives that thrashed all of us about, turbulently.

Voice tone of silk in the key of magic, strumming our synapses,
Like that old guitar she played, always missing that last string,
Chording emotions out of melodies, kissed into the microphone
That night, when she reluctantly agreed to sing one more.

She must have waited all night, holding the trump card song,
Until the end, singing others, slowly breaking us down,
Melting defenses against listening, delaying her penetration,
Past those heart walls, thick as mountain fog on an autumn morning.

Voice tone of silk in the key of magic, lyrics resounding from her tongue,
Absorbed by our wounded and injured souls, consoling
Lives that thrashed all of us about, stilling the turbulence
Just for a few moments during that, almost unsung, last soothing song...

Spiritual People

Spiritual people are those who listen well,
Who have learned to listen to messages that others seldom hear.
Spiritual people are searchers for meaning and purpose,
Seeking to discover important messages in the events and happenings
Of ordinary and extraordinary days.

Spiritual people strive to be in touch and in harmony
With their spirit: the innermost aspects of themselves.
They understand that to know their own spirit,
They must know and commune with others
And with the Great Spirit: God.

Spiritual people understand that ultimately they have little control
Over the events and people in their life, and in time they grow to accept that
Everything is in order according to some unknown higher plan.
However, they believe that always they have control of their choices
In responding to people and events.

Spiritual people strive to accept life as it is
Surrendering as much as they can
Their desires for life to be otherwise,
Yet spiritual people dream and share visions
Of a better way and ultimately a better world.

Spiritual people accept their imperfections
As a confirming part of their humanity.
They celebrate the fact that they do not have to
Be perfectly or do perfectly.
Spiritual people accept these truths in others, also.

They seek others from whom they can learn and grow,
And they are most drawn toward others to whom
They can relate in authenticity and sincerity.
Spiritual people believe that the Great Spirit brings people
In and out of their lives when it is time and when they are ready
To learn the truths that the relationship can yield.

Spiritual people believe that ultimately
All answers are within and that each experience,
Whether pleasant, neutral, or painful,
Is concealing a gift
Which can be discovered
If they listen
As spirit...

117

Dream Meeting With An Elder Spirit

Days come, days go.
Drenching rain, melting snow,
Thunder claps, lightning blinds;
Earth is dying; no one minds.

Grass of green, flowers of red;
Courting disaster was all he said.
Laughter piercing, silence ending;
Strangers arrive, cultures blending.

Moon is ending, sun arriving;
Ocean waving, tides subsiding.
Short is the year, long is the day;
Dreams of it changing, all I can say…

The Tribe Of The Circle

Drumming circles beckon
From campfires encircled
By searchers and seekers
Who searched and sought
In other places, in other ways;
Conclusions always the same:
What was missing?
Connexion and direction.

One night I sat in a circle,
Smoking the pipe with my brothers and sisters,
Inhaling and exhaling my prayers:
To the hope of the East,
The passion of the south,
The cleansing of the West,
And to the mystery of the North.
I exhaled my prayers to the Father Sky
To oversee my journey,
And to the Earth Mother
To guard my steps,
And I inhaled the goodness
Of the Great Spirit
And exhaled my gratitude for His creation.

This is the Tribe of the Circle:
A sacred circle of fire and mystery.
The heartbeat of the drum
Guides us inward and empowers us outward,
In journeys beyond time and reality,
Where the medicine heals the wounds,
Relieves the pain, awakens the dreams,
And summons the spirits to join us
In our quest for illumination and vision.

This is the Tribe of the Circle:
A sacred circle of fire and mystery,
Where the heartbeat of the drum
Guides us inward for direction,
And outward for connexion…

Elders Walk Among Us

The coiled serpent fascinates me,
Intrigued by his novelty,
Watching him uncoil,
I follow him down a broad path,
That constricts to a narrow passage,
I can barely walk upon,
Faltering left or right,
Without balance,
Without freedom.
I cannot return to the path's beginning,
Having walked it this long.

Give me a meadow without fences,
Streams with no dams,
And mountains to climb,
That do not narrow at the top,
Where I can walk along the treetops,
Clothed in red,
And dance with the unseen elder spirits,
Who rattle the leaves when Wind visits,
Perched as a daytime, sleeping owl,
Awaiting the darkness' silent freedom flight,
Where I can abandon the constricting snake path.

Light is still far more blinding,
Than the revelations in the darkest midnight.
Elders walk among us, through fields of forest green,
Spirits from seven ages carry us, present but unseen,
Intimated in the daylight with the kind turns of Fate,
And in the darkness, guiding us with ancient wisdom,
During sleep time, unveiled in irrepressible dreams…

Native America – 1992

So, now 500 years have painfully passed,
Since the ships arrived on our shores,
Bringing many new people so different, so fast,
Who hurt us, betrayed us and brought many wars.

Stealing our land and mocking our traditions;
Delivering us their illnesses; horrible reservation conditions.
Many children died; many grandparents stopped dreaming.
The oppressions from these people, endless lies and scheming.

We signed treaties that were broken,
Believed words they said were not spoken,
And when they ceased hurting us, we hurt ourselves badly:
Drank too much, believed too little, and lived so sadly.

But 500 years later, we have still survived.
Our people are great in number; our spirits revived.
Though many died without reason; many atrocities done.
The Trail of Tears is over; Trails of Strength have begun.

Our sacred drums beat on, loud and true.
We still tell our story…
Our celebration dances continue.
We walk with honor and glory.

We respect and thank the four sacred directions.
We cherish our families; maintain our connexions.
Tribal traditions are honored; our prayer smoke still rises.
Great Spirit still listens; Grandmother Moon recognizes.

Five centuries later, we are still here,
Growing in number with each passing year;
Drumming and dancing like never before.
Look to Father Sky; the eagle still soars.

Prouder and freer, our people stand tall,
Like mighty oaks of the forest, we will never fall.
The spirits of our ancestors laugh loudly these days,
Rejoicing with us as we honor and believe in our ways.

Our customs and traditions, viewed by some as wrong,
But five hundred years later, we are still going strong:
Drumming, singing and dancing with feather;
The Fire of the Indian burns brighter than ever…

They Cannot Hear Our Drum

Though they may attempt to modernize our red hearts:
Cut our braids of tradition and power,
Traded for crew cuts and white-man jobs.
Turn our sacred sweat lodge into New age saunas
Led by self-proclaimed, reality-denied shaman healers.
Document our ancestors' paths and agonizing histories
In white-washed books distorting the truths
Our elders died on Tearful Trails to maintain.
Tell us education is an asset and will help our People,
But how can they teach our children Red Roads
They have not traveled and cannot comprehend?

There are worlds beyond what they see,
And red ways deeper than they can fathom.
They may train the earth's animals to do their tricks,
Or glue a stone to a chain to convert a rock into a pet,
But have they listened to these wisdom-keepers?
Have they learned from these ancient ones?
Have they felt their silent and inspiring power?

Our Red World is different from theirs:
Where White Buffalo Woman is more than a legend;
Tepee and chikee are more than dwelling places;
Where Fire gives more than heat and food;
And Feathers free more than birds to fly.

Though they may attempt to modernize our red hearts;
Our hearts will never turn away from the distant drum,
And we will die braided, smudged, and blessed
To enter the spirit side where elders dwell
Becoming another campfire in the night sky:
One of many infinite stars reminding all red children
That our ancestors are always with us...

Winds of Disconnexion Blow Dust In Our Eyes

Alone within the city;
Alone among the People.
Winds of disconnexion
Blow dust in our eyes,
Blinding us to who we are,
Hiding the vision
Of all we once knew.

Winds of disconnexion
Blow dust in our eyes,
Particles of dirt from the cities'
Fragmented growth called progress;
Pieces of dust from wise elders,
From tribes extinct and languages lost.

We are cultures without memories,
And people who have forgotten our relations.
We squint our eyes
To see our brother;
We blink at the dust
To recognize our sisters.
We squint our eyes
To find our ancestors,
To unearth the mysteries buried;
Buried with the dusty, closed eyes
Of the Old Ones who knew
That Red Road is to be traveled,
Not in disconnexion, but together.

Yesterday at the ceremonies,
An elder man walked up to me,
Squinting his eyes,
Handed me his lighter
To kindle his cigarette,
As the dusty wind blew,
He said, "I'm too old,
I cannot see so well."
I lit his tobacco in windy silence.
Straining to look at my face,
But Grandfather could not see his Grandson.
He turned and slowly walked away
With the Dust of grief in his eyes,
And the Winds of disconnexion on my face…

Careless World, Leave Me Alone

Careless world, leave me alone.
I requested food; you gave just a bone.
My spirit unnourished by what you withhold;
I walk with gentility in a world too cold.

There is hatred that permeates this place I am in,
Such that soul-murder is rampant wherever I have been.
The currency of Now is blood-stained with pain,
Walking over anyone on their way to great gain.

I am weary of this world, lacking from greed
To get ahead at any price, no matter who bleeds
From soul-piercing wounds leaking pieces of my heart.
Sure… it would be great to change it, but where should we start?…

Unpacking A Life That Used To Be

Sitting in the middle of her new apartment living room,
Surrounded by boxes that contained a life that used to be.
Saddened by a love that once seemed right—now wrong;
She wanted out, but now ached with grief at the death of a promise.

Always meticulously organized, she wished all the boxes unpacked,
But understood it would take time to rearrange the contents
Into drawers and unfamiliar cupboards, onto shelves and tables.
Still, she wanted everything unpacked and rearranged in short time.

One box at a time, she unpacked, placing clothes in her new closet,
Recently purchased food in her new refrigerator and cupboards,
One box at a time, she unpacked, putting pictures and memories into drawers,
Including those wedding pictures and souvenirs from her life that used to be.

And, as she unpacked those boxes, her grief lingered in the room,
Sometimes as a sad cloud looming over her joy;
Sometimes like a clinging vine with a stranglehold on her heart,
With moments of esteem-lowering guilt for losing a love she once promised.

Just like those boxes that contained a life that used to be,
All the containers of grief cannot be unpacked in an instant,
To be positioned on the shelves that contain her life.
She learned to unpack her pain one grief box at a time.

One day, in time, arriving home from work, she smiled,
Walking in her apartment, carefully noting its arrangement
Pleased with her new home no longer cluttered by the untidy boxes,
Pleased with her life no longer cluttered by the unfinished grieving…

Instinct To Survive

On this gray-clouded morning, as the crisp air
Chilled the damp leaves, awaiting the sun's drying,
A blue bird with bread in her beak
Is perched on a vine-adorned power line,
Only a few feet away from an energetic squirrel,
Moving in the other direction with food in his mouth.
The animals awaken in the morning, gathering food
To return to the young ones, instinctively.

Hundreds of miles away, a man awakens
In a storm-shelter, barely last night escaping
The strong winds that destroyed his family's home.
In another part of the world, a soldier awakens,
Protected in a tank, where sleep is interrupted
By gunshots and small bombs, exploding outside,
Where he protects the freedoms of my country,
And wonders about his newborn daughter,
Whom he has yet to meet, at home with his young wife,
Praying again to some God that he hopes exists,
That he hopes will retrieve and save him,
From this nightmarish world,
Where survival is a dream,
And instinct is fear.

Life in the mornings awakens, with demands to survive:
Animals feed their young; men rebuild destroyed homes,
And soldiers keep enemies at bay, fighting to return to family,
On crisp air mornings, when gray clouds disperse,
Opening for the healing, reliable sun to chase
The remainder of last night's darkness away,
Instinctively…

Ghost From An Affair

Like some ghost through the door,
Imagining her walking in again,
Where he returned to their diner,
Watching from his seat,
Sitting at that familiar table,
Their meeting place for those talks,
The ones that left him resuscitated
From a life of memories that took his breath.

Driving away, she had questioned herself
That night, pulling in her driveway,
She doubted herself and her choices...
Yesterday's and tonight's.

Entering her home, he kissed her,
Jarring her from her ponderings,
Rattling her back to this reality,
The commitments, the obligations.

Settling in her wedding bed,
She felt safe with her husband,
Though confused with
Earlier evening events.
Why question what she had?
Why tempt fate with desire?

And in that sleepy stillness,
Beyond awake, before dreams,
She imagined herself walking
Ghost-like, through a door,
At their meeting place,
Smiling at him seated
At that familiar table...

Excerpts From A Wounded Heart
(or Open Heart Surgery Without Anasthesia)

Stay strong, my friend, when the world shatters your back,
With a load that would break a Clydesdale down.
I have known adversity before,
And stared in the face of the angry and hurting ones
Who couldn't find the words to say: I need you.

Long ago, Someone wrote this story out,
This book that maps out my path,
I just wish I could get a copy of that damned script!
Or am I writing this one with a borrowed pen,
One I can't remember where to return?

The broken-hearted roam in and out of my life
Seeking solace and comfort from my own,
Breaking further that part of me that never had the time to heal.
It's all wrong somehow, how much the injured ones continue to injure.

Vicious cycle of the victims becoming the criminals,
Harming those who have appeared for helping,
Scratching vindication across scars that rise up on one's body,
Like a part of their soul wants to leave their skin.

I cannot tell you that the future will be good,
Or even if you or I will be in it.
What we have is today and this moment
Of reading and listening to our own heart's opening.

Opening one's heart is a sure way to break it,
But in turn, breaking is a sure way to open it,
And caring connection is that elusive bird that only lands
On an open and safe island that is prepared for it to arrive.

I know that your picture of the future is mostly blank-screened;
I only wanted to know if you saw me walking across that screen,
Sometime, somewhere in the fast-approaching tomorrows.
Don't worry; you will never have to ask me to leave,
Sad that you will never understand why I left before you arrived
That day to tell me that our time had expired.

Like a cold mortician, cleaning up a dead man,
She drained me, filled me with mortifying fluid parts of her,
Fixed me up just right with the proper attire,
Secured my eyes closed, and sewed my lips together.

Don't watch this, and don't speak.
I just want to position you correctly in this comfortable box,
Like a mortician, cleaning up a dead man,
She vacuumed my heart of its contents.

Question is: why do I think so little of myself?
I wasn't a victim; hell, I volunteered!
Now let me pull away, withdraw from you,
Climb back into my own scarred skin,
Try to patch with some logic and understanding
Those holes you left in my heart,
Pry open these eyelids and untie my mouth;
There are things I must see again,
And words too heavy to remain on my tongue…

Days Like My Life Continue Passing By Me

Days, like my life,
Continue passing by me
Rapidly,
Like that sunrise I tried
To photograph in the desert one evening,
On a cloudy day in the summer,
I drove west of Speedway Boulevard
Toward Gate's Pass,
Racing the setting sun
Around curves and narrow roads
Clouds billowed about,
Arranging themselves
For a picturesque calendar,
Frame-worthy shot,
But just as I arrived,
Racing with equipment,
Setting up to take that perfect picture,
The last third of that orange ball
Went into overdrive,
Dropping succinctly below the horizon,
And I missed it.
So close,
Everything in place,
Almost…
Until the opportunity disappeared,
Just below the horizon
Of that evening's perfect chance.
Days, like my life,
Continue passing by me…

Some Live Their Lives

Some live their lives as water,
Like a mountain stream
Gently flowing down the path
Which does not resist,
Detouring as needed around rocks and trees,
And other various and sundry obstacles.

Some live like roaring, monotonous ocean waves,
Breaking in and sliding out,
Controlled by the damming sand,
And some unseen atmospheric force
Miles away from the breaking waves.

Some live their lives as smoke,
Being sucked in and exhaled out by others,
Slowly killing those who inhale it,
Annoying those exhaled upon,
Only yielding a subtle, temporary exhilaration.

Some live their lives as wind,
Which knows not its origin or destination,
Only that it is,
And that it fluctuates
From still and lifeless
To gentle, calming breezes,
To forceful and destructive gusts.

I want to live as lava,
Unlike gentle streams apologetically detouring their paths,
Unlike waves with the damming sand's control,
Unlike smoke sucked in and breathed out by others,
And unlike the wind without stability and destination.

I want to live as lava,
Gushing forth from the mother volcano,
Being born as an infant with a burning desire to move,
Anxious and steaming to trek a path
Wherever I will, with no need to detour or avoid,
Until I, like lava, am nothing but cold stone
With this notable difference:
My stone bears my chiseled name and two dates
And perhaps these eternal words:
"He lived his life…

Forever Altering The Course Of Our Lives

One morning while driving across the Bronston Bridge,
I tossed an apple core from my open Jeep window
Having consumed its meatier parts.
The apple core bounced against the abutment on the bridge,
Back out into the roadway, I noted glancing in the rearview.
Forty-six vehicles and seven minutes behind me,
A lonely and attractive, single mother of two children in elementary school
Was driving speedily across the Bronston Bridge late again for her meagerly waged job,
Distracted as she attempted to cell phone her complaining supervisor,
Glanced at the apple core in the road, altered by glistening bright sunlight in her eyes,
Mistook the apple core to be an abandoned puppy, and swerved quickly
Into the side of a car of a teenage boy driving to school for his Algebra final examination.
Both drivers braked solidly, bumping and grinding, side against side, banging twice against
The bridge abutments and back again into the other's car, until nervously and without injury
Screeched to a stop, delaying all the traffic behind them.
One observer quickly alerted 911, who dispatched a traffic officer in fewer than four minutes.
The recently divorced officer, one year shy of 40 arrived, exited his patrol car,
Directing the shaken drivers to pull their wounded, but operational cars to the side,
As his partner directed the awaiting, observing vehicles to carry on to their destinations.
The officer approached the two drivers, startled to see his newly-licensed teenage son,
Frightened, but unharmed in one of the wounded vehicles.
He had not seen his angry son, since his separation seven months ago,
And had longed to see him again.
The father officer, joyful his son was unharmed, opened his arms,
Embracing a son too frightened to be angry, relieved to be held safely by his daily-missed father.
The officer resumed his role, documenting the accident, consoling the kind woman
Who mistook the apple for a puppy, and completed his report,
Impressed with the kindness of the woman at fault in the Bronston Bridge accident.
She asked to speak with him later in the week... for the report,
To which the officer smiled, and assured her that he would be available... for the report.
She pulled away with crinkled fender and misshapen door to another workday she dreaded,
As the officer drove his son rapidly, blue lights spinning, on time, to his final Algebra exam.

I am ever fascinated with the vast redirection one's life can take
When the seemingly tiniest of happenings occur.
There really are no accidents!
Everything I do, large or small,

Beside a friend or even miles in front of any stranger,
Could easily alter the course of his fate for all his days to come.
Thus, I must tread lightly, carefully and thoughtfully beside those I know,
And in front of those I have yet to meet, and trust always that Fate
Will take even the things I toss aside to connect and reconnect lives
Onto pathways fated for each to walk upon and grow upon.

Days and weeks move on with the smallest of items
Forever altering the course of our lives.
Months later, the officer and his son would never again resume their silences,
That neither ever wanted from the start, and the boy had Aced that algebra final,
Testing with a confidence that only a father's assuring long-awaited presence could create.
The woman who mistook the apple core for a puppy in the glistening sunlight
No longer works at the dull, meagerly paying job,
Not since she and her boyfriend began living together last July:
The officer she met one day after her accident on the Bronston Bridge.
Their children: her two elementary school children, and the officer's teenage son
Greatly enjoy the new happy home and family, especially with the new puppy their parents
Brought home last month as a surprise and early Christmas present.
They named the puppy…
Apple…

But... I Was Only Listening

I have listened to the cries of those
Whose lives lacked and yearned for more;
Listened to detailed accounts of those
Whose hearts were broken by fear and desperation;
Heard the brooding worries of those
Whose minds plagued them with unsquelchable pessimism;
And I have seen the disillusionment of those
Whose young dreams became old and distant.

And,
I have wondered if my hearing and empathy
Mattered;
Wondered if my words of intended comfort and guidance
Mattered;
Wondered if in the great scheme of things,
A few ill-spoken mutterings of consolation and counsel
Really mattered at all...

This morning Richard asked the secretary
If he might see me for but a moment of unscheduled time.
As he entered my office with a more confident visage,
I abstractly recalled our prior sessions:
His hurt, detailed accounts, worries, and disillusionments;
My listening, empathy, counsel, and ill-spoken mutterings.

He sat in the same chair and began:
"I stopped by to say, 'Thank you'.
Good things are happening in my life now;
I owe much of that to you."
With a few more strokes from him,
And some poor attempts at humility from me,
Richard departed my office,
Leaving me in wet-eyed awareness that
In the great scheme of things,
Perhaps to one important life,
I had
Mattered...

Searching Outside, Awakening Within

I have struggled to find my way,
Searching the paths of those who have gone before.
There are those who adopted an old way.
There are those who created a new one.

Sifted through parental messages,
Discarded the malarkey,
Trying to adhere to the useful.
I have read at least as many books
As the rest of those who search,
Pondering the wisdom of the sages of old,
Pondering the meanings of the gurus of today.
Sometimes they all say the same thing;
Sometimes they all say the same nothing.

It is exhausting living beneath the shadows
Of my own wisdom,
Feeling lost in a darkness of my own creation,
Believing others outside me possess the light,
And if only I could formulate the right questions,
I would finally receive the long-awaited answers.

Then one morning
I awakened
To my destiny,
And knew…
That all life had to offer…
Could be…
Mine…

I Do Not Know The Pain You Feel

I do not know the pain you feel.
I run from my own, sometimes, and what it might reveal;
Have tried to make some sense of a derailed life;
Struggled to integrate events that cut like a knife
Through some idealized script I was trying to live,
But paradise and perfection are seldom what this world gives.

I do not know the pain you feel,
Though I have tried to care and comfort and heal.
Your wounds are deeper than I can see;
I can only know your pain's meanings you share with me.
At times, you wish for me to patch a wound I have not been shown,
Or remove a pain-filled cancer within you that I have not grown.

Maybe there are no skilled surgeons of the soul,
And fumbling along to comfort slightly is the only possible goal.
Maybe there are no absolute healers of the heart,
And attempting a little patchwork as we listen is doing our part
To care for those we love when they walk through crippling pain.
I am sorry the umbrella I held for you did not keep off all the rain…

Acknowledgments

"Corners of Madness" was previously published in <u>Poetry In the Woods, Second Anthology</u>, in 1990, Ft. Lauderdale, FL: East Coast Academy of Poets.

"Native America—1992" was previously published in <u>The Seminole Tribune</u> on February 15, 1992, Hollywood, FL: Tribal Council of the Seminole Tribe of Florida.

"Two Men at the Bar" was previously published in <u>Poetry In the Woods, Third Anthology</u>, in 1992, Ft. Lauderdale, FL: East Coast Academy of Poets.

Quotes on page vii:

Nietzsche, Friedrich, (1955), <u>Beyond Good and Evil</u>, Chicago, IL: Henry Regnery Company.

Jarre, Kevin, (1993), <u>Tombstone</u>, movie from Hollywood Pictures, and directed by George Cosmatos. Dialogue between Doc Holliday (Val Kilmer) and Wyatt Earp (Kurt Russell).

Printed in the United States
by Baker & Taylor Publisher Services